What is BEST *for* AMERICA?

It's Our Country It's YOUR Choice

Winning Strategies,
Thoughts & Inspirations

ROAD SCHOLAR PUBLISHING GROUP

RANDY E. KING

Left – Center - Right, What is Best for America?
Winning Strategies, Thought & Inspirations
©2011 CEG, LLC.
Published by
Road Scholar Publishing Group, LLC.
Scottsdale, Arizona USA
Reboh@cox.net

All rights reserved. No portion of this book may be reproduced without the written approval from Road Scholar
Publishing Group.

Disclaimer

This publication was designed to give the reader information on the subject matter covered. It is sold with the
understanding that the publisher and author are not engaged in giving legal, accounting or other advice out-
side the field of the author's expertise. If other kinds of professional advice are needed, please seek competent
professionals in those fields.

It is not the purpose of this book to claim that this is the only book on the subject. The reader is urged to read
all books on the subject and to learn as much as possible.

Anyone who decides to follow the advice given in the book must do so with all due diligence.

Every effort has been made to cover and research all aspects using the author's own experiences. However, there
may be mistakes both typographical and in content. The purpose of this book is to educate and entertain. The
author and Road Scholar Publishing Group shall have neither liability nor responsibility to any person or entity
with respect to any loss or damage caused, or alleged to be caused, directly or indirectly by the information
contained in this book.

If you do not want to be bound by the above, you may return this book to the publisher for a full refund.

Visit: www.randyeking.com / www.storiesofusa.com
Other books by Randy E King:
• Grow Your Company Grow Yourself, Together Dominate the Market Place.
• Legacy Leadership, Leading Yourself and Other to Greatness. It all starts with YOU!
• The Victory System for Career Change.
• American Pride, by and for our young Americans!

You can email the author: rking23@cox.net or call: 1-800-913-1359

Publisher's Cataloging-in-Publication Data
    King, Randy E.
        Left center right : what is best for America? : it's our country it's your choice :
        winning strategies, thoughts & inspirations / Randy E. King. -- 1st ed.
        p. cm.
        LCCN 2010940175
        ISBN-13: 9780615416991
        ISBN-10: 0615416993
        1. Political participation--United States. 2. United
        States--Politics and government.   I. Title.
        JK1764.K56 2011   323'.042'0973
                    QBI10-600247

Edited by: Linda Jacqueline Reboh
Cover Design: Dream Graffx, www.dreamgraffx.com
Interior Layout: Fusion Creative Works, www.fusioncw.com

Printed and bound in the United States of America

Dedication

This book is dedicated to every American that goes the extra mile to ensure the legacy of our great nation, so that it can continue to be passed on to generation after generation. To my father, a great Patriot, his love for America was renowned. My mother and I miss him more and more with each passing day. To my wife Linda, for her continued love and support during all of my writings, I love you more today. And to my good buddy Steve for sending me the email that got me "fired up" to write this book. Mike Beaumont, what a brilliant and talented person, our meeting was meant to be. The Freedom Academy staff and students, it always starts with a dream. Miso for letting us use his picture, and to all of my friends for putting up with "How does this one look?" Thank you God for giving me the strength and wisdom to hear the calling to write this book.

A very special dedication to my friend Gary Rossman; America was founded on what this man possesses: Courage, Strength, Positive mindset and an overall never give up attitude.

*"He who knows nothing is closer to the truth
than he whose mind is filled with falsehoods and errors."*
—Thomas Jefferson

From The Author

As I was finishing up the final touches on this book, I came across an article that I found very interesting. Being very familiar with how the business association world works when it comes to raising huge amounts of cash, I thought this would be some great information for you to read. Everyone within the media will say and do anything that will expand their audience.

Rush Limbaugh and many others have had their best two years off the negativity of the American people. The former chief of staff Rahm Emanuel said Limbaugh is "the voice and the intellectual force and energy behind the Republican Party."

Yes, the Left wants you to follow them. The Right wants you to do the same. How about you follow YOU! They are not smarter than you. You can have the same information that they have. And if you really want to, make up your own mind based on, well, once again you. Let's get into that article that I ran across. (Newsweek 11/08/10) This is great stuff!

The most influential political figures are the ones that make the most money. Conservatives like Rush Limbaugh come in number one with an annual income of $58.7 million and a weekly audience of 15 to 20 million people according to "Talkers Magazine." Glenn Beck, $33 million with an audience of 11 million according to Newsweek. Sean Hannity- $22 million with a similar audience and Bill O'Reilly- $20 million with 3 million viewers nightly. John Stewart - $15 million. Sarah Palin- $14 million from books and paid speeches. Don Imus - $11 million. Keith Olbermann - $7.5 million. Laura Ingraham - $7 million. Stephen Colbert - $ 5 million. Arianna Huffington - $5 million Mark Levin - $5 million. Chris Matthews- $4.5 million. Bill Maher - $4 million. Jorge Ramos - $4 million. Joe Scarborough - $3.5 million. Rachel Maddow - $2 million. And finally, Ann Coulter - $750,000. Did you wonder why Ann Coulter a right winger was appearing on Bill Maher?

One final note: You can gage the Business Association's bank accounts and the media's bank accounts from the political party who is running the White House and who is control of the House and Senate. It is BIG business at the expense of our children and what is truly best for America.

Contents

Introduction	9
1. Politics – Policy and your Personal Philosophy	13
2. Leading the No Excuse Life	29
3. The Three C's	37
4. The Rules of Conduct	41
5. American Pride Series –	49
Part 1 – Adults	51
Part 2 –Young Americans (children)	71
6. Thirteen Most Patriotic Speeches	
Ronald Regan – "Farewell Address to the Nation"	89
Martin Luther King – "I Have a Dream"	100
Franklin D. Roosevelt – "Pearl Harbor Address to the Nation"	106
Winston Churchill – "Blood, Toil, Sweat, and Tears"	108
Theodore Roosevelt – "The Right of the People to Rule"	110
General Douglas MacArthur – "Duty, Honor, Country"	124
John F. Kennedy – "The Decision to Go to the Moon"	131
Patrick Henry – "Give Me Liberty or Give Me Death"	138
Ronald Reagan – "Remarks at the Brandenburg Gate"	142
George Washington – Farewell Address	151
Franklin D. Roosevelt – First Inaugural Address	171
John F. Kennedy – Inaugural Address	177
Abraham Lincoln – Gettysburg Address	182
7. Developing Your Foundation	185
8. Developing the Wings to Soar in America	195
9. Inspirations & Thoughts	205
10. The World Came to See America	221
11. Green Tree Theory – Dumb Leaders vs. Smart Leaders	229
12. Definitions and Terminologies	233
13. Great Quotes About Our Great Nation	241
14. Discovering Your American Dream	253
15. Ten Greatest Entrepreneurs	271
16. Twenty- Steps for Success & Twenty Six Top Characteristics of Successful People	277
17. Politics and Young Americans –They are the Future	289
18. Great Achievements by Teenagers	301
19. Realizing What You Have	307
20. What is Next for America?	311
About the Author	317

Introduction

"Knowledge and Awareness does not have a political party. In most of our schools however, this is not the case. Our true enemy is ignorance and apathy. I don't know and I don't care attitude will break America. This book is about your personal awareness of the Past – Present – Future & the Inspiration to keep America Great"
—Randy E. King

About seventeen years ago I decided to write and produce a program entitled: *"Rediscovering the American Dream, It Hasn't Changed Have You?"* While I was writing the lecture series for the program, I felt motivated and inspired, because I recalled that only seven years prior I was broke and slept in my car, but through hard work, focus, discipline and a positive attitude I accomplished everything I set out to do.

What was going on all those years ago that is different from what we are facing today? Nothing. Sure, the stock market will fluctuate, and yes, the economy has shifted, but as Robert Babson, an investment adviser who predicted the 1929 crash, claimed the markets were driven by Newton's third law of motion: Every action has an equal and opposite reaction.

The American people are still the same, so is the ability to do what we need to do to make our American Dreams a reality; anything is still possible in America.

Is this a motivational book? Well, if it gets your head out of the negative thinking then, yes it is.

This book is full of inspirations and encourages your self-evaluation, so that you take personal responsibility for your life. Most importantly, the purpose of this book is in my desire for a better America to ensure a stronger future for our children. This book is about becoming politically aware; making our own decisions based upon your own knowledge of what is right and wrong, and not on the opinions of the so called pundits in the media world. Knowledge is power. As you read this book, I want you to THINK about, "*What is Best for America?*" I know the American people can make well informed decisions about our future, if they are not manipulated by the media, or influenced by our elected officials or candidates who make unrealistic promises.

All the books I have written over the years have been about personal development through the utilization of personal knowledge. Whether it was improving how you run your business, advancing in your current career, or becoming a leader who leaves a lasting legacy. My goal has always been to provide the knowledge that my readers required to accomplish and fulfill their dreams.

When I began to write this book, I was partly inspired by the age old question: "What will our lives look like five or ten years from now?" I want to put this question in another way: What will the American Democracy look like in five or ten years? Our

Founding Fathers laid out our democratic system with hopes of a better future for its people. We are in that future now; it is in our hands. Are we preserving our founding fathers legacy the way they imagined it?

This is not a doom and gloom book. I am not a doom and gloom kind of guy. But I do want us to start asking that very important question. *"What is Best for America?"* And how can **WE** champion the cause and inform ourselves as to who and what is best for this country?

Democrats, Republicans, Independents and all religious denominations, everyone in our country can benefit from reading my book. Together, we can restore our *AMERICAN PRIDE,* and if I can touch just a few people who read this book then I have **gone the extra mile**.

Individual responsibility must continue for America to remain great, and achieving success in our country is the crown of democracy and freedom.

> *"He who would accomplish little must sacrifice little.*
> *– He who would achieve much must sacrifice much.*
> *– He who would attain highly must sacrifice greatly."*
> – James Allen, *As a Man Thinketh*

Chapter 1

Politics – Policies and Understanding Your Personal Philosophy

"Those who stand for nothing fall for anything."
—Alexander Hamilton

This chapter is dedicated to those people who are confused about the issues; who should I vote for, or on which side of the political spectrum should I lean toward. During many of my speeches I give around the country, I am often confronted by people asking the same question: "Which politician is right and which one is wrong?"

Young adults still in school find themselves with this same dilemma as the adults in this country. In my early days with a large business association, I would look at a particular legislative issue and weigh out both sides to see what was best for the United States. It was very informative and thought provoking to be able to look at both sides of a piece of legislation and make up my own mind. Making up one's own mind on what you believe takes knowing what your personal philosophy is. What will affect you directly and what will affect America as a country can come down to your personal philosophy.

Personal Philosophy:

1. The Constitution, have you read it? – go to www.storiesofusa.com
2. America overall
3. Success and failure
4. Less or more Government in your life
5. Social and environmental
6. Taxes
7. Freedom
8. Independence

Developing your personal philosophy in these areas will set your "Sails" in place. Your personal philosophy is your personal guidance system in life. What do you stand for? What do you desire to accomplish within your life? And more importantly, what don't you want. How many people do you want controlling your outcome and looking over your shoulder?

I truly get a kick out of people trying to sell me on what their personal belief system is. Can you have a personal philosophy and a separate business philosophy? Yes! I have seen this many times. But if you do not have personal integrity you will not have business integrity. Hard to separate. Once again, I don't want to persuade you as to the adjustment of your "sails of life." You can probably tell by reading my bio and getting to know me through my lecturing and reading my books what my business, political and personal philosophy is.

My philosophy of life and business "sails" were shaped when I was sixteen years of age and then firmly planted at nineteen. At sixteen I needed a car to get back and forth to work. My father said to me, "I am going to get you a car, however I will co-sign for the car and I hope you miss a payment, because I like that little car." I never missed a payment, dad was not going to get that car and he knew it. A little reverse psychology looking back. He was teaching me financial independence, I knew I could only depend on my own resources for the things I wanted out of life; nothing was going to be given to me I had not earned through my hard work.

Visiting my mom and dad, at nineteen years of age, I can remember dad pulling out a huge roll of money (looked big to me at the time I was broke) he looked at me making sure that I saw his large amount of money, he firmly stated, "Son if you don't give me grand- babies I am going to cut you out of my will."

I can remember this like it was yesterday. I very confidently and firmly said "Dad you can keep your money." Looking back, it amazes me how quickly and with no hesitation I responded to his suggestions. I saw I would have to earn whatever success was out there and would never do what I didn't want to do just for money. I became at the age of nineteen my own person. I could not be tempted to do another person's will for money. This shaped me into becoming the independent thinker that I am today. I also saw what inept parenting could do to a young person.

Parents, help your children understand what works in life, how to be independent; how to work hard to achieve what they want and help them set goals. Teach them to respect their bodies and their minds. Ask them how they feel on important issues, this will serve them well when it counts.

Do I have to worry about the adults? You bet I do. A good friend of mine said to me, "Dumb parents will often raise dumb kids." Hmm! He can be pretty intense when it comes to the outcome of our youth and I don't blame him.

Parents should teach their children the attributes of what constitutes a right and wrong philosophy. Show them the areas where people have developed the wrong philosophy and how their lives did not end up the way that they wanted. Both sides of the coin must be understood. I always use the lottery analogy. If I gave an individual business owner a sum of money, what would the results look like within five years? Some will grow the opportunity and some will mess it all up within those five years. Over 30% of the lottery winners end up broke and in bankruptcy after five years. Why, because they have the wrong philosophy.

Having a personal philosophy will help you decide your political positions, such as: who to vote for, what to vote on, and how to keep America moving forward as a strong country. You cannot have a democracy when the people who vote are not educated. As Alexander Hamilton said in the beginning of this chapter, "Those who stand for nothing fall for anything."

American Independent Party

The American Independent Party is a right-wing political party of the United States that was established in 1967 by Bill and Eileen Shearer. In 1968, the American Independent Party nominated George C. Wallace as its presidential candidate and retired Air Force General Curtis E. LeMay as the vice presidential candidate. Wallace ran on every state ballot in the 1968 presidential election, though he did not represent the American Independent Party in all fifty states; in Connecticut, for instance, he was listed on the ballot as representing the "George Wallace Party." The Wallace/LeMay ticket received 13.5 percent of the popular vote and 46 electoral votes.

In 1969, representatives from 40 states established the American Party as the successor to the American Independent Party. In some places, such as Connecticut, the American Party was officially constituted as the American Conservative Party. (The modern American Conservative Party, founded in 2008, is unrelated to the Wallace-era party). The official party flag adoption took place on August 30, 1970. The flag depicts an eagle holding a group of arrows in its left talons, over a compass rose, with a banner which reads "The American Independent Party" at the eagle's base. In 1972, the party nominated former Congressman John G. Schmitz of California for president and Tennessee author Thomas Jefferson Anderson for vice president. In 1976, the American Party split into the more moderate American Party, which included more northern conservatives and Schmitz supporters, and the American Independent Party, which focused on the deep South. Both of the parties have nominated candidates for the presidency and other offices. Neither the American Party nor the American Independent Party has had much national success.

The American Independent Party has had ballot status in the state of California since 1968 and is still active there. As of early 2008, AIP's registration total was 328,261.

In the early 1980s, Bill Shearer led the American Independent Party into the Populist Party. Since 1992, the American Independent party has been the California affiliate of the national Constitution Party, formerly the U.S. Taxpayers Party. However, in 2008 one faction of the AIP broke with the Constitution Party and gave the ballot line (which it controlled) to Alan Keyes, candidate of the similarly-named America's Independent Party.

Many political analysts have theorized that the Party, which has received very few votes in recent California elections, maintains its state ballot status because people join the Party mistakenly believing that they are registering as an "independent," also known as a "non-partisan" or "decline-to-state" voter. One such voter was Jennifer Siebel, fiancée of San Francisco's liberal Democratic mayor Gavin Newsom; in 2008, Siebel attempted to change her party affiliation from Republican to Non-Partisan, but "checked the American Independent box thinking that was what independent voters were supposed to do," according to the San Francisco Chronicle.

Democrat Party

"Democrat Party" is a political epithet used in the United States instead of "Democratic Party" when talking about the Democratic Party. The term has been principally used by conservative commentators and members of the Republican Party in party platforms, partisan speeches and press releases since the 1930s. The explicit goal is to dissociate the name of the rival party from the concept of democracy.

Democratic Party members and non-partisan individuals have objected to this modification. New Yorker commentator Hendrik Hertzberg wrote:

There's no great mystery about the motives behind this deliberate misnaming. "Democrat Party" is a slur, or intended to be – a handy way to express contempt. Aesthetic judgments are subjective, of course, but "Democrat Party" is jarring verging on ugly. It fairly screams "rat."

In similar two-word phrases, the word "Democrat" may also become controversial when used as a substitute for "Democratic" (as in "Democrat idea" or Senator Bob Dole's reference in a debate to "Democrat wars"). Sometimes this renaming is objected to as a misuse of "Democrat" as an adjective.

The history of the term has been traced by scholars to the 1940s. The earliest known use of the term, according to the Oxford English Dictionary, was by a London stock-market analyst, who wrote in 1890, "Whether a little farmer from South Carolina named Tillman is going to rule the Democrat Party in America – yet it is this, and not output, on which the proximate value of silver depends." The term was used by Herbert Hoover in 1932, and in the late 1930s by Republicans who used it to criticize Democratic big city machines run by powerful political bosses in what they considered undemocratic fashion. Republican leader Harold Stassen later said, regarding his use in the 1940s, "I emphasized that the party controlled in large measure at that time by Hague in New Jersey, Pendergast in Missouri and Kelly-Nash in Chicago should not be called a 'Democratic Party.' It should be called the Democrat Party."

The noun-as-adjective has been used by Republican leaders since the 1940s and appears in most GOP national platforms since 1948. In 1947, Republican leader Senator Robert A. Taft said, "Nor can we expect any other policy from any Democrat Party or any Democrat President under present day conditions. They cannot possibly win an election solely through the support of the solid South, and yet their political strategists believe the Southern Democrat Party will not break away no matter how radical the allies imposed upon it." President Dwight D. Eisenhower used the term in his acceptance speech in 1952 and in partisan speeches to Republican groups. Indeed, in the early 1950s the term was widespread among Republicans of all factions.

In 1984, when a delegate of the Republican platform committee asked unanimous consent to change a platform amendment to read the Democrat Party instead of Democratic Party, Representative Jack Kemp objected, saying that would be "an insult to our Democratic friends." The committee dropped the proposal. In 1996, the wording throughout the Republican Party platform was changed from "Democratic Party" to "Democrat Party". In August 2008, the Republican platform committee voted down a proposal to use the phrase "Democrat Party" in the 2008 platform, deciding to use the proper "Democratic Party". "We probably should use what the actual name is," said Mississippi Governor Haley Barbour, the panel's chairman. "At least in writing."

Republican Party

Abraham Lincoln was the first Republican President of the United States (1861–1865). Founded in northern states in 1854 by anti-slavery activists, modernizers, ex-Whigs and ex-Free Solders, the Republican Party quickly became the principal opposition to the dominant Democratic Party. It first came to power in 1860 with the election of Abraham Lincoln to the Presidency and oversaw the American Civil War and Reconstruction.

The first official party convention was held on July 6, 1854 in Jackson, Michigan. The Republicans' initial base was in the Northeast and the upper Midwest. With the realignment of parties and voters in the Third Party System, the strong run of John C. Fremont in the 1856 Presidential election demonstrated it dominated most northern states. Early Republican ideology was reflected in the 1856 slogan "free labor, free land, free men." "Free labor" referred to the Republican opposition to slave labor and belief in independent artisans and businessmen. "Free land" referred to Republican opposition to plantation system whereby the rich could buy up all the good farm land and work it with slaves, leaving the yeoman independent farmers the leftovers. The Party had the goal of containing the expansion of slavery, which would cause the collapse of the Slave Power and the expansion of freedom. Lincoln, representing the fast-growing western states, won the Republican nomination in 1860 and subsequently won the presidency. The party took on the mission of saving the Union and destroying slavery during the American Civil War and over Reconstruction. In the election of 1864, it united with pro-war

Democrats to nominate Lincoln on the National Union Party ticket.

The party's success created factionalism within the party in the 1870s. Those who felt that Reconstruction had been accomplished and was continued mostly to promote the large-scale corruption tolerated by President Ulysses S. Grant ran Horace Greeley for the presidency. The Stalwarts defended Grant and the spoils system; the Half-Breeds pushed for reform of the civil service. The GOP supported business generally, hard money (i.e., the gold standard), high tariffs to promote economic growth, high wages and high profits, generous pensions for Union veterans, and (after 1893) the annexation of Hawaii. The Republicans supported the pietistic Protestants who demanded Prohibition. As the Northern post-bellum economy boomed with heavy and light industry, railroads, mines, fast-growing cities and prosperous agriculture, the Republicans took credit and promoted policies to sustain the fast growth. Nevertheless, by 1890 the Republicans had agreed to the Sherman Antitrust Act and the Interstate Commerce Commission in response to complaints from owners of small businesses and farmers. The high McKinley Tariff of 1890 hurt the party and the Democrats swept to a landslide in the off-year elections, even defeating McKinley himself.

Theodore Roosevelt, 26th President of the United States (1901–1909).After the two terms of Democrat Grover Cleveland, the election of William McKinley in 1896 is widely seen as a resurgence of Republican dominance and is sometimes cited as a realigning election. McKinley promised that high tariffs would end the severe hardship caused by the Panic of 1893, and that the GOP would guarantee a sort of pluralism in which all groups would benefit. The Republicans were cemented as the party of business, though mitigated by the succession of Theodore Roosevelt who embraced trust busting. He later ran on a third party ticket of the Progressive Party and challenged his previous successor William Howard Taft. The party controlled the presidency throughout the 1920s, running on a platform of opposition to the League of Nations, high tariffs, and promotion of business interests. Warren G. Harding, Calvin Coolidge and Herbert Hoover were resoundingly elected in 1920, 1924, and 1928 respectively. The Teapot Dome scandal threatened to hurt the party but Harding died and Coolidge blamed everything on him, as the opposition splintered in 1924. The pro-business policies of the decade seemed to produce an unprecedented prosperity until the Wall Street Crash of 1929 heralded the Great Depression.

Dwight Eisenhower, 34th President of the United States (1953-1961).The New Deal coalition of Democrat Franklin D. Roosevelt controlled American politics for most of the next three decades, excepting the two-term presidency of Republican Dwight D. Eisenhower. African Americans began moving toward favoring the Democratic Party during Roosevelt's time. After Roosevelt took office in 1933, New Deal legislation sailed through Congress at lightning speed. In the 1934 midterm elections, 10 Republican senators went down to defeat, leaving them with only 25 against 71 Democrats. The House of Representatives was split in a similar ratio. Republicans in Congress heavily criticized the "Second New Deal" and likened it to class warfare and socialism.

The volume of legislation, and the inability of the Republicans to block it, soon elevated the level of opposition to Roosevelt. Conservative Democrats, mostly from the South, joined with Republicans led by Senator Robert Taft to create the conservative coalition, which dominated domestic issues in Congress until 1964. The Republicans recaptured Congress in 1946 after gaining 13 seats in the Senate and 55 seats in the House.

Ronald Reagan, 40th President of the United States (1981–1989). The second half of the 20th century saw election or succession of Republican presidents Dwight D. Eisenhower, Richard Nixon, Gerald Ford, Ronald Reagan, George H. W. Bush and George W. Bush. The Republican Party, led by House Republican Minority Whip Newt Gingrich campaigning on a Contract with America, was elected to majorities to both houses of Congress in the Republican Revolution of 1994. The Senate majority lasted until 2001, when the Senate became split evenly but was regained in the 2002 elections. Both Republican majorities in the House and Senate were held until the Democrats regained control in the mid-term elections of 2006. In the 21st century, the Republican Party has been defined by social conservatism, a preemptive war foreign policy intended to defeat terrorism and promote global democracy, a more powerful executive branch, supply-side economics, support for gun ownership, and deregulation.

Have you ever thought about why you're a Democrat, or a Republican, or a Libertarian, or a Green? If someone asked you what party you belonged to and why, out of nowhere, would you be prepared enough to respond, assuming you consider yourself to be of a certain party? If someone asked you if you believe in everything the Democratic Party stands for, as an example, would you be able to say yes with absolute certainty? Do you even know all of the platforms that the Democratic Party even pursues? What about the Republican Party; are you absolutely sure that you know about all of the positions they represent?

Sometimes it's baffling that someone would pick one or two issues and then go with a party on those issues alone, as if there are no independents or other parties that take the same exact stances on those issues. The reasons that explain these occurrences simply do not satisfy me, such as aligning yourself with the same political party as your parents. You need to take a step back, and analyze your parents' position carefully. Do you know why they vote for a certain party? Are you of the same alignment because their ideas are firmly engraved into your brain? Maybe. It does not have to be this way, but it happens a lot. Otherwise it's due to ignorance, I mean how many people can claim that they know all of the party's platforms and their stances. My guess would be not many, and I would be right.

The two big shots, the Democrats and the Republicans, are backed by the people as well as corporate interest. It's true. They pull in a lot of money from donations, it's simply not fair. People often vote for only these two because people feel like voting for anyone else outside of these two parties is a waste of a vote. No one should ever feel like their vote is being wasted, ever. Why should there only ever be two candidates we can vote on and not feel like the other candidates are a waste of time? The world is not in black and white. The world is not one way or the other, it's simply not true. There are not only two opinions on any matter.

Let's not argue about the different colors within each party; we all know that these two parties are virtually in the center when you look at the grand scheme of political alignments. So the question becomes, will these two parties be from now until forever the only two "choices" that America really has, or is the public eventually going to do its research and vote for their truly best match?

With the advent of the Internet, it's simply inexcusable not to know what the major party platforms are, as well as the platforms of independent candidates and the minor parties. So many hours of the day are spent, wasted away from surfing the web. Why not do a Google search on Ralph Nader? Don't take a look at just what you disagree with him on, take a look at his entire platform. His beliefs on all issues is what's important, because come election time you're not going to be able to pick just the one or two viewpoints you agree with, you have to take along the entire bag of ideas each candidate carries. If you're a financial conservative, but disagree with the war, are you willing to forfeit that disagreement to get the financial policies that you'd like? That is the kind of question that everyone should be struggling with.

But, the people hardly ever are torn in this manner. How can that be? How can so many people agree on the exact same ideas on every issue? It's not probable. I wouldn't want a country whose population thinks the exact same things anyway, because then there's no debate, there's no questions asked, and there's no criticism. People need feedback, without it, people continue to make the same stupid mistakes or the same sorts of actions that could be corrected or improved. Right now, the Democrats correct the

POLITICS – POLICIES AND UNDERSTANDING YOUR PERSONAL PHILOSOPHY   27

Republicans, and the Republicans correct the Democrats. But what if they're both wrong? Who's correcting the both of them?

I urge you to take a look at the different platforms that exist in the United States. Do a Wikipedia search on all of the major political parties and then on some of the other independent candidates. Get to know where you truly stand on the issues and which party satisfies a particular issue the best. Then decide where your alignment truly is. No stupid online quiz is going to be able to tell you what party you belong to, it's nonsense. It would take a very long time for a quiz to know absolutely how you feel on every possible issue. It's hard for a quiz to know how you feel about even a single issue! Feelings are hard to use as empirical data. Only you can know where you are on the political spectrum.

Knowledge is power here, and the power to change the political climate in the United States I think should be a powerful motivator for anyone. Why should anyone pick the better of two evils? Why can't someone pick the best candidate for their own views? Why should two parties influenced heavily by lobbyists control what the American people want? Why do people have such a poor view of government? Could it possibly be because they were forced to choose a candidate they did not much want, because they wanted the other candidate even less?[1]

Chapter 2

Leading the No Excuses Life!

"The price of greatness is responsibility."
—Winston Churchill

I am sure you have heard the phrase, "Be careful what you ask for, you may just get it." Let me illustrate this for you through two separate stories.

Rick and James were both recently laid off from their jobs. Rick sits at home, watches TV, complains about not having any money, hopes that he will soon get his job back and feels sorry for himself.

James gets up early the next morning, puts on a nice suit and tie, drives over to the office of the sales manager of the company that was a client of the corporation that he was just laid off from. James explains to the manager that with his knowledge of the industry, wealth of experience and willingness to work hard, he is a valuable asset.

If you refuse to accept your circumstances and take action you will usually get what you want. But you must have the work ethics to acquire the things in life that you want. If all of us would get up and work at just 80% of our capacity most companies would be light years ahead and you would have everything that life has to offer.

Before the owners of any company decide to manufacture their product or sell their service, they think of the idea long and hard before they decide to invest their hard earned dollars into the project. They're offering the good opportunity. And if the good opportunity is good enough for them to invest their hard earned dollars in, shouldn't we take advantage of the opportunity as well; especially if all we have to do is invest our efforts, hard work and time.

Let me share another story with you. One of my employees at the time gave me a call. This guy had a lot of potential. He called me on the phone and said, "Randy, I want to apologize to you, the reason I'm not succeeding is because I can't keep focused."

This was a 45-year-old man telling me that he couldn't keep focused. I said, Robert, let me give you a little example of not keeping focused, you have two lovely children, and let's say they go to a very expensive college down the road......let's say Harvard, you invest money in them and they've invested time, and one day they call you and they say, Dad, I'm flunking out. Your first question is going to be "Why are you flunking out?" And they say it's because they can't keep focused. How many kids in this country would love to go to Harvard? And yours "blew it," because they can't keep focused. What are you going to say? Who's to blame, the opportunity, or the individual?

His comment, of course, was not pleasant. Reality checks are not always pleasant. Then I said, "Let me talk to your wife." He said, "No way, Randy!" He knew better and he understood the point. If all it takes is focus, then I'll buy you the eyeglasses, the binoculars; whatever it takes.

Excuses are something that I don't buy in my organization and I don't want you to buy them either. I don't want you to listen to excuses anymore and I don't want you to give them. Look at yourself in the mirror and ask yourself, "Am I doing everything that I can possibly do to maximize my efforts today?" If the answer is "no," then change; if the answer is "yes," and you're still not getting what you want out of life, change the opportunity; that's okay.

There are a lot of great companies and there are a lot of entrepreneurial people *starting their own* businesses. This country was founded on the concept of free enterprise. There's *no* reason that you can't have it; it's out there. If your current opportunity is not good enough, you can always create your own. I want to stop here and give you some facts and figures about the world of small business. I am as you can tell a huge fan of our small business community.

As you have heard me say many times throughout my book, small business is truly the engine that drives America. Small firms accounted for 65 percent (or 9.8 million) of the 15 million net new jobs created between 1993 and 2009. Much of the job growth is from fast-growing high-impact firms, which represent about 5–6 percent of all firms and are on average 25 years old.[2]

How important are small businesses to the U.S. economy?

Small firms:

- Represent 99.7 percent of all employer firms.
- Employ half of all private sector employees.
- Pay 44 percent of total U.S. private payroll.
- Generated 65 percent of net new jobs over the past 17 years.
- Create more than half of the nonfarm private GDP.
- Hire 43 percent of high tech workers (scientists, engineers, computer programmers, and others).
- Are 52 percent home-based and 2 percent franchises.
- Made up 97.5 percent of all identified exporters and produced 31 percent of export value in FY 2008.
- Produce 13 times more patents per employee than large patenting firms.[3]

How do regulations affect small firms?

The smallest firms (fewer than 20 employees) spend 36 percent more per employee than larger firms to comply with federal regulations. The disparity is greatest in two areas: very small firms spend four and a half times as much per employee to comply with environmental regulations and three times more per employee on tax compliance than their largest counterparts.[4]

What is the role of women, minority, and veteran entrepreneurs?

Of the 27.1 million nonfarm businesses in 2007, women owned 7.8 million businesses, which generated $1.2 trillion in revenues, employed 7.6 million workers, and paid $218 billion in payroll. Another 4.6 million firms were 50 percent women owned. Minorities owned 5.8 million firms, which generated $1 trillion in revenues and employed 5.9 million people. Hispanic Americans owned 8.3 percent of all U.S. businesses; African Americans, 7.1 percent; Asian Americans, 5.7 percent; American Indians and Alaska Natives, 0.9 percent; and Native Hawaiian or other Pacific Islanders, 0.1 percent. Veterans owned 2.4 million businesses in 2007, generating $1.2 trillion in receipts; another 1.2 million firms were 50 percent veteran owned. About 7 percent of veteran business owners had service-connected disabilities in 2002.

In 2008, the overall rate of self-employment (unincorporated and incorporated) was 9.8 percent, and the rate was 7.1 percent for women, 7.2 percent for Hispanic Americans, 4.7 percent for African Americans, 9.7 percent for Asian Americans and Native Americans, and 13.6 percent for veterans. Service-disabled veterans had lower self-employment rates than non-service-disabled veterans.[5]

Get into a business that can get you where you need to be, but don't make the excuses. "No excuse management" is what I tell managers. Just like the new cadets at "West Point," we should only answer questions in one of four ways: "Yes, sir!" "No, sir!" "No excuse, sir!" or, "I don't understand, sir!" It's called "No Excuse Living."

Accepting responsibility is something that I drill into the minds of people who are around me on a day-to-day basis. After all, we are not paid by the quality or the quantity of our excuses, but by the "bottom line." It's called "results." Remember, Discipline weighs ounces, regret weighs tons. Do it now. Make it happen.

There is a rule and I want to change it. And I want you to help me to change it, but it's going to take a long time. And if I can change it, then I've done my job. It's going to take your help as well. It's called the "80-20 rule." It's called, "*some will, some won't*, **so what**?" I speak to a lot of winners and I talk to a lot of people about the "80-20" rule.

About a month ago a woman came up to me and said, "Randy, hey, great seminar, but the challenge is, in my organization "*some will, some won't, so what*?" And I said, "We have got to change that, because if you're part of the "*some won't*" and the "*so what*?" category, you're in trouble."

There are very few "*some wills*," and we've got to change that. I want to add something to your life today. I want to give you the information that will inspire you to become part of the "*some wills*;" because 80% of the results are being brought in by 20% of the work force in your company. Think about this! It's as old as I am. It's as old as you are. It's a fact folks, that 80% of all results are generated by 20% of the people in your company; 80% of the wealth in this country is generated by 20% of the population.

That's okay if you're part of the 20%, but it's not if you're part of the 80%. I want you to try to shoot over to the 20% to have

80% of the goodies. Ninety-seven percent of the actors in the Screen Actors Guild make less than $10,000.00 a year. Now don't ask me why; it's just one of those things. Here's another figure: 97% of those people who retire, retire on less than $13,000.00 a year in income. Remember the 5 million sales people…..less than 1% make a living folks, and we've got to change this "80-20 rule." Will you help me? I know you will.

We all want to succeed and we all want the "wealth of life," but we're not always willing to work for it. We're always looking for shortcuts. If the lottery hit $50,000,000.00 and only one outlet sold tickets, and it opened up at 4:00 a.m., and the news media made the comment that tickets would be sold out by 9:00 a.m., I guarantee you that the majority of you would be there at 4:00 a.m. trying to buy those lottery tickets.

I'm an optimist, I'm not looking for shortcuts to success, first, because the odds are against it from happening, and second, if there is an easy way out, the chances are I'm not going to hang onto it. I'd squander it away: Remember 30% of the lottery winners end up broke and in bankruptcy five years after they win the lottery. Don't let people control what you do. You control it.

If someone around you is having a bad day, tell them, "Hey, I don't want to be part of it, I'm going off to bigger and better things." Most people don't like winners. I teach people that there are three groups that basically want you to succeed: Your company, your family, and you. How many of you, when you have a bad day, a bad week, or you possibly get into a slump, do you look at your manager and say, "Hey, I need help."

Again, your ego can trip you up, but you've got to put your ego in your back pocket, and do not be afraid to ask for help.

Figure it this way, if you're failing and you don't seek help, who's to blame? The only time I hear from people is when they have a great day, but the ones who are champions, the ones who are winners when they have a bad day or a bad week guess what they do? They call me. They call the support group.

Remember the story about the guy who wanted to get someone to give him a wake-up call to get him out of bed to get him going? What if someone doesn't show up, this guy's in trouble. Remember, the inability to get up in the morning is not an excuse, a lot of us need to get a different type of alarm clock; it's called a "reality check" clock.

I believe that "God doesn't make junk." So, don't give me the excuse that someone else is better than you, because I don't *buy* that story. If that's the case, then go out there and become better than they are. You've got to *get* the books, CD's, and go to the seminars, get a fitness program. Go to professionals who understand how to dress you and how to cut your hair. I'm a tyrant when it comes to the basics, I see so many people that miss the basics, the little things in life and business that make the big stuff happen. Do not be one of those people who choose to remain average. And always remember;

IF IT IS TO BE, IT IS UP TO ME

Chapter 3

Three C's - Being Successful in America

"The greatest danger for most of us is not that our aim is too high and we miss it, but that it is too low and we reach it."
—Michelangelo

Share the next two chapters with your children and their teachers.

Parents and teachers can "mess" it all up for our children who are our future leaders if they do not have an understanding of the next two chapters.

I believe that you can do well in any economy if you apply what I am going to tell you. If you have read my book, you have read many stories of rags to riches- this is my story also. I came to live my life through my Three C's years ago.

When I was consulting with a large advertising company, the CEO and I became good friends. Our value systems matched the way we viewed our responsibility to employees and the independent contractors in his company.

He wanted to move on and find his replacement. He and I

had lengthy discussions on who would be the "Right" person. He agreed that I was the "Right" person for the CEO spot. But, I needed to make sure I was the "Right" person as well. I mentioned to the CEO that we should bring in an executive coach to help us with the decision.

After months of searching for the executive coach who was a good fit for us, the process began. The Coach asked me probably one of the toughest questions that I ever had to deal with: He said, "Randy, write down why you have done so well in business and what do you think you owe your success to?" After literally weeks of not being able to clearly define why I have been successful, I came to believe that even if you asked most pro athletes why they hit that shot or hit that ball, their answer might be, "It just comes natural," but I knew that was not the answer the coach was looking for.

My answer finally came to me: My Three C'S. I had a moment of euphoria. "I GOT IT, I GOT IT," I shouted. "That's it!" I now want to share what, 'I Got' with you. It is simple: My Three C's are Character, Communication and Commitment to excellence.

As I travel around the country and give my lectures and motivational talks, I always leave my audience with my Three C's.

It's amazing to me after people listen to my P.R.I.D.E. CD series they always remember the Three C's. I truly believe that if we teach our children the Three C's and we live by them, we will have a great life, not only in business, but in our personal life as well.

The first C is Character. This is the fundamental foundation of all of them. The granddaddy, the big Kahuna – if you miss this one you need to crawl in a hole, go away and resurface after you have fixed this big C. If you don't have this one, your kids, your family, and your business life will suffer from mediocrity. You will be labeled mediocre; a big mark on your forehead. Character is who and what you are when no one else is looking. It's going back to the cashier when she gives you too much money in change. Character is the stuff that makes a strong leader; it's not only doing the "Right Thing," it's doing what is Right ALL THE TIME. You can have very little talent and lack all the skills to have a good life, but if you are a person who possesses a strong Character you will develop the talent and hone the life skills to become a success in your life. What a great legacy to leave to your children, to be passed on generation to generation.

The second C is Communication. This is a skill that is required to do well in business and life. You must master not only good, but great communication skills. This skill can be taught and mastered to perfection. I have always believed that the world is not run by the academics, but by the great communicators. Study history and you will find the giant leaders of this great nation all had the ability to move mountains with their communication abilities. It is truly the "art of persuasion" at its best. This is a very powerful skill to possess. Over time, it has and always will be, used for the good and unfortunately for evil as well. This is why the first C of Character must be in place before moving on to the second C. It is a truism; you will get 90% of what you ask for when you ask well.

The third C and equally important as the other two is COMMITMENT TO EXCELLENCE. When I ask my audience how well should your children do? Easy answer, ALL THAT THEY CAN! Why would we as adults do anything less, fall short of the mark? Could of, would of, should of? You have got to be kidding me, leave it better then you found it. I write my books, produce my CD's and lecture around the country, because I believe that anything is possible in America. The foundation of this country was founded on flat out going for it ALL, ALL OF IT; never backing down, going for it and getting everything that is yours. Not what you deserve, but what you have skillfully and competently created for your life. Whatever it is you do, do it well and do it all. I have seen many times in hotels, the bellman who becomes the General Manager.

I have seen a homeless man on a five year educational plan (no, not college but 5 years to get through high school) two dollars in his bank account, become a millionaire by forty, running his own companies, authoring books, CD's series and lecturing at major universities on leadership topics. If this person can do it so can YOU. But you must master my Three C's. "You can do well in any economy if you bring extraordinary value to the market place, do it better than your competition, do it better than any person before you; do it better than the person sitting next to you." This is America, anything is possible. When you, work hard at what you do, and more importantly work harder on yourself.

Chapter 4

Rules of Conduct - Then & Now

"When ancient opinions and rules of life are taken away, the loss cannot possibly be estimated. From that moment, we have no compass to govern us, nor can we know distinctly to what port to steer."
—Edmund Burke (1729-1797) British political writer

While writing this book some portions of it were spent in the public library. I noticed when I first walked into the library, "Rules of Conduct" was posted on the wall. After reading the document I smiled and thought; "This has to be a part of this chapter." I want to thank the Scottsdale public library for this document. I asked myself, why did this document need to be there in the first place? This is a very upscale library in a high end area of North Scottsdale (Arizona). These simple and straight forward "Rules of Conduct" should apply to all of us, young and old in all walks of life.

I also have Thomas Jefferson's "10 Rules of Conduct" that was written in 1825. I found this very insightful and I included it in this chapter. Once again, as I have stressed throughout my book, there are some basic rules of "conduct" that need to be followed to insure a positive and successful America for many generations to follow, these are "time tested," PASS THEM ON.

My Public Library "Rules of Conduct"- 2011

Be considerate and respectful of all users and staff, and behave in a manner that does not disturb other persons. Unacceptable conduct includes, but is not limited to:

1. Loud, disruptive and inappropriate behavior that would be annoying to a reasonable person using this library
2. Damaging or stealing property
3. Sleeping
4. Use of tobacco products
5. Possession of firearms, weapons or illegal substances
6. Treat library property with respect
7. Dress appropriately. Person whose bodily hygiene is offensive so as to constitute a nuisance to other persons shall be required to leave building
8. Supervise your children and assist them in observing appropriate conduct
9. Silence your cell phone
10. Leave bicycles and gasoline-powered vehicles outside
11. Personal items are not to be left unattended. Carry or keep items with you at all times. The library is not responsible for items left unattended
12. Comply with staff request on regard to library policies
13. Assistance dogs are the only animals permitted in the library

Noncompliance with the Rules of Conduct may result in expulsion from the Library and/or suspension of library privileges.

THANK YOU FOR YOUR COOPERATION

Thomas Jefferson's Rules of Conduct -1825

Wisdom to Apply in "Practical Life"

His ten commandments of practical life include when to talk if upset: "When angry, count ten before you speak; if very angry, a hundred." (Jefferson to Thomas Jefferson Smith, 21 February 1825.)

Ten rules that Thomas Jefferson believed were essential for leading a fulfilling life. According to the Jefferson Encyclopedia, these were compiled at the request of a father who had named his baby son Thomas Jefferson Smith. They were pared down somewhat from an earlier list Jefferson sent to his granddaughter, Cornelia Jefferson Randolph.

1. Never put off till tomorrow what you can do today.
2. Never trouble another for what you can do yourself.
3. Never spend your money before you have it.
4. Never buy what you do not want, because it is cheap; it will be dear to you.
5. Pride costs us more than hunger, thirst and cold.
6. We never repent of having eaten too little.
7. Nothing is troublesome that we do willingly.
8. How much pain has cost us the evils which have never happened.
9. Take things always by their smooth handle.
10. When angry, count ten, before you speak; if very angry, a hundred.

Qualities of a good parent

The only way to raise a special human being is to become one....

1. Raise your children by example, example and example.
2. Tell them you love them and then love them – everyday.
3. Tell them they are the most important things in your life.
4. Spend quality time with them. One on one.
5. Instill self-confidence in them.
6. Teach them right from wrong.
7. Teach them to respect others.
8. Be their best friend.
9. Praise them every day.
10. Show them affection. Hug them often.
11. Be a role model for non-violence.
12. Listen to them.
13. Take the boredom out of their lives by joining them in adventurous, fun activities.
14. Talk to them about drugs, gangs, sex, alcohol and peer pressure. You will get to know where they stand on these very important subjects.
15. Show and guide your kids by modeling good behavior.
16. Don't take drugs in their company.
17. Respect them.
18. Don't judge them harshly. They will make lots of mistakes just like you did when you were their age.
19. Don't humiliate, insult or embarrass them in front of others.
20. Take an interest in their education as it is one of the most important things that will impact greatly on their future.

QUALITIES OF A GOOD TEACHER

Empathy

You have the ability to bond with your students, to understand and resonate with their feelings and emotions. To communicate on their level. To be compassionate with them when they are down and to celebrate with them when they are up.

Positive Mental Attitude

You are able to think more on the positive and a little less on the negative. To keep a smile on your face when things get tough. To see the bright side of things. To seek to find the positives in every negative situation. To be philosophical.

Open to Change

You are able to acknowledge that the only real constant in life is change. You know there is a place for tradition but there is also a place for new ways, new ideas, new systems, and new approaches. You don't put obstacles in your way by being blinkered and are always open and willing to listen to others' ideas.

Role Model

You are the window through which many young people will see their future. Be a fine role model.

Creative

You are able to motivate your students by using creative and inspirational methods of teaching. You are different in your approach and that makes you stand out from the crowd. Hence the reason why students enjoy your classes and seek you out for new ideas.

Sense of Humor

You know that a great sense of humor reduces barriers and lightens the atmosphere especially during heavy periods. An ability to make your students laugh will carry you far and gain you more respect. It also increases your popularity.

Presentation Skills

You know that your students are visual, auditory or kines-thetic learners. You are adept at creating presentation styles for all three. Your body language is your main communicator and you keep it positive at all times. Like a great orator you are passionate when you speak. But at the same time you know that discussion and not lecturing stimulates greater feedback.

Calmness

You know that the aggression, negative attitudes and behaviors that you see in some of your students have a root cause. You know that they are really scared young people who have come through some bad experiences in life. This keeps you calm and in control of you, of them and the situation. You are good at helping your students de-stress.

Respectful

You know that no one is more important in the world than anyone else. You know that everyone has a place in the world. You respect your peers and your students. Having that respect for others gets you the respect back from others.

Inspirational

You know that you can change a young person's life by helping them to realize their potential, helping them to grow, helping them to find their talents, skills and abilities.

Passion

You are passionate about what you do. Teaching young people is your true vocation in life. Your purpose in life is to make a difference.

Willing to Learn

You are willing to learn from other teachers AND your students. Although knowledgeable in your subject you know that you never stop learning.[6]

Chapter 5

American Pride Series

Part One - Adults
Part Two - Children

There are two chapters in this American Pride section: One for adults and one for children. The adult version is a lecture that I give around the country and is also available on CD. I kept the lecture in its original version with few corrections, so it would keep its hard hitting effect. When you write books you're at the mercy of your publisher and editor. Things can become so polished they lose the author's effect he wanted to create for his readers.

The children's version was a lot of fun. What I liked about the children's version of the American pride series was it was created 100% by our young Americans.

American Pride, It's Our Country It's Our
Choice - Making a Difference Everyday

Part One – Adults

I want to welcome you to "American Pride: It's Our Country,
It's Your Choice – A Journey of Meaning, Thought and Inspiration;
Making a Difference Every Day in America."

I'm excited to be here today. I put together this Pride series
because I believe in our great country. We have a great nation.
Our American flag, if held it up to the light, is starting to be less
fibrous, more see through. Our flag the symbol of freedom is
starting to unravel right before our eyes; I want to make sure that
we stop the unraveling and I know you do too.

I've been in the promotion of the free enterprise system for
twenty-three years. Fourteen of those years I spent with a major
association as a senior leader. Currently I am President and CEO
of my own company; we do the promotion, and enhancement
for industries in the free enterprise system.

American Pride is an ACRONYM. It's about thoughts, mean-
ings and inspiration. So together, let's go down this path have fun
and take a look at our AMERICAN PRIDE. There are certain
words and phrases that will touch your emotions. Let's take this
journey together and start off with the **A** of our American Pride.

The first **A** is America – we love her. We protect her, we die for her and we do whatever it takes to protect our freedom and individuality.

Going back to the transparency analogy of our American flag. I can't believe we have a debate going on right now as to what America stands for. Our country was founded based on the free enterprise system and the basic Judaic/Christian beliefs of our great nation. But part of living in a Democracy is having different opinions and the freedom to express those opinions even if we disagree. Then of course we make up our own minds after we have heard all sides and have educated ourselves. There can be no debate though that our country was founded on these basic freedoms: Freedom of speech, Freedom of enterprise, Freedom of religion.

Another A - abilities – this is probably one of my favorite. I have achieved who I am today, because of my own abilities. No one else showed me or told me what I could or could not do. This was based on my efforts, my hard work and my personal abilities. On a sobering note, I keep my old checkbook in my car to remind me where I have come from – it showed a $2.00 balance, broke, obviously couldn't rub two nickels together, lived in my car for literally 30 days, until I was able to get out there put things together, which turned around my life! Once again – **only in America can you rise from nothing and become somebody by your own efforts.**

Achievement is also another A of our American Pride. Our achievements come from our hard work and efforts we put forth to have the things we desire. However, achievement can come in many different forms: Making a lot of money can be one level of achievement, having a solid spiritual foundation, family foundation, among others. Being able to appreciate all that you have, going for it in America and, feeling good about who you are and what you have achieved, is called gratitude for living in America.

My next **A** of our American Pride, is abundance. We have abundance. We live in an abundant America. In America there is a tremendous amount of abundance, based on your abilities and based on your attitudes as well. Attitude is how you react to a situation and not on the situation.

Many years ago, in September to be exact; I lost my mother-in-law, my father, my dog and I was diagnosed with type 1 diabetes. So in the month of September, I was absolutely what I called "snowed over." Everything depended on my attitude on how I would handle what life had thrown at me all at once.

Attitude is really defined in four areas to give you an idea of how I look at attitude. Like four seasons, there is winter, summer, spring and fall. I know a lot of you would like to say, "No, Randy, I don't want any winters, I just want the summers springs and I'll take two falls," but that can't happen. You have to have the winters because the winters make you stronger for the other winters that will come around and besides they make you appreciate the good when the bad happens to you, and when the winters do come back around, you have a mindset, you're prepared for it, you have a mental toughness and you've actually dressed a lot warmer and are able to endure, the coldness the darkness that has set into your life for a few weeks or months. I've been there, I've had long winters, I've had months where I thought I'm never going to get myself out of this so called snowstorm that I'm involved with. So attitude is very important. The old cliché is attitude determines one's altitude. It is true, attitude will get you through life, it really will.

M's of our American Pride. The areas that come to mind are our mentors and our moms that make a difference. Before I get to the moms and to our mentors, I encourage each of you, to do me a favor; make a difference today. Let me say it this way – however you found it put it back better; because the giving starts the receiving process. At the end of the day, make a difference not only for yourself, but more importantly for someone else.

Let's go over to our mentors for a second because the mentoring program is very important in America. You're not going to get to the next level by yourself', it's not going to happen, I am not where I'm at today by being a loner. I started off years ago with my father as my role model, he obviously was a very good man. He was a very strong principled individual and he really laid out a good foundation for who I am today and what I'm about (I talk about this later).

Another important mentor in my life was a gentleman I met at the age of nineteen. I walked into his small business and I asked for a job and he said, "Randy, I'll employ you but you must work thirty days without pay and at the end of thirty days I'll see how well you're doing and maybe I'll put you on payroll." Three years later, I was running his multi-million dollar business. So, his mentorship and my father's mentorship meant a lot in my growth and who I am today.

The mentor process is something you need to have; outside advice from individuals that you trust and respect can be a big help. It's very important that we make sure that the advice we're getting is not from someone whose own life is messed up, so just be very cautious with whom you surround yourself with; I call it your personal board of directors. The more mentors you have on this board: Individuals with diverse backgrounds who can give you different spins, different ideas and different thoughts; this is very important to your growth and success.

I was at a leadership retreat in which I was facilitating two months ago and I was confident that if we took the fifteen different problems that were in the room and we threw them up on a blackboard and took the four most damaging problems we were facing, that within a matter of a couple hours, we could put it together to solve those challenges. In this group of individuals, they had the skill set to resolve all the challenges once they brainstormed. So make sure you get a good mentor, mentee system in your life.

Next in the **M's is** moms, we love you. Ladies, this is for you. I've always said this; you have this chip in your brain. You've got this intuition. Women and moms have intuitions. You have this ability to see things that we guys just can't see. I remember a story many years ago of a mom and dad they are upstairs and the kids are in the other room and mom in bed with dad and they're asleep and mom jumps up and says, "There's something wrong, there's something wrong," dad says, "Honey, go back to sleep, there's nothing wrong, everything is ok." Then mom says, "No, I know there's something wrong." She goes downstairs, sure enough, the latch is off and the window was left unlocked. Advice to you, men, when it comes to your moms and your wives – I've been with my wife for 23 years, put your ego in your back pocket, put that testosterone on the back burner. Women and moms I applaud you, keep doing whatever you're doing to keep this country great.

E of our American Pride. Several things come to mind, obviously – education, eradicate hate, economics and enterprise. I want to talk about education for a moment, because it is very important that our children are taught well in school. There are some schools and some universities that are teaching the opposite of what this great country was founded on. It comes down to real basic economics as to what drives this economic engine: small business, fewer taxes, less regulations. Do not mandate a healthcare program on small business It will kill them! – If you remove the barriers within the small business community, they're able to do several things: (1.) Create jobs. (2.) Create profits. This in turn will create lifestyles for the families of the employees that work in small businesses.

It's not the large corporations. Large corporations are sucking the life out of us. I own a small business; I cannot go to the federal government for a bailout. If my products and services do not meet the standard of marketplace, they do not get sold.

Here's a simple rule to live by; how you'll do well in any economic time, it's simple: bring extraordinary value to the marketplace. If the auto industry cannot make cars that Americans want to buy, they need to re-design their cars. It is as simple as that. The government cannot take care of you. They'll mess it all up in the long run. I get intense on this because I am an entrepreneur. I started with $2.00 in my pocket and now have my own business. I was on the five year plan, that's five years in high school, not college. It took me five years to get through high school, school was not one of my favorite activities, the marketplace was where I needed to be. I've written several books, I've written CD programs, I've written best practice programs for several major industries; I am a self-educated man. Education is very important, but we have to make sure that we get the right message to our children about what and who runs this country; everything is possible in the great U.S. of A.

Eradicate hate is another part of the E within American. I measure people, by what is inside their heart, how they react to life. We're in a time now where a racial debate is taking place at a national level. I think we need to stop doing this because I'm a firm believer: United we stand, divided we fall. Let's get this thing figured out and let's erase hate. Let's quit using this hate program as a crutch and let's move forward, because if I can do this – a man that was homeless, penniless, without a formal education – I certainly know you can do the same.

I was driving to a place of business to give one of my lectures and a song came on the radio: David Bowie's, back in 1972 entitled, "We Were Young Americans," and there's a phrase in that song that really caught my attention, it kind of goes like this, "Do you remember President Nixon? Do you remember the bills we had to pay, even for yesterday?" Now we are, obviously, creating tremendous debt in this country that we're going to pass along to our children. I'm afraid, that a young me coming up, that's eighteen or nineteen years of age, is not going to have the same freedoms and the same opportunities that I did. I'm going to continue to fight that they do have the same opportunities and I hope you will fight with me, I know you will because this is America, and we all love this country.

We're going to finish off the **E** because it's about enterprise. Enterprise, small business is the engine, not being redundant and I don't think I can say this enough, is what runs this great country. What a great country we live in, to be able to sit there on the side of the road me and my friend Jason spot a cricket on the side of the road and we grab that cricket and many more. Put a sign up that says, "Bait for sale: three crickets for a dollar." Five years later, we have five or six locations throughout the country! As simple a business concept as that is. The entrepreneurial spirit cannot be stifled, it must be encouraged, we must continue to support and continue to tax less, and put fewer regulations on small businesses.

Let's now move over to **R** of our American Pride, we're half way through this great journey together. I hope you're enjoying it, I know I get a kick out of this because it really does make us think about what we're doing, who we are and where we're going and we can't give up folks, we've got to keep going. In the **R** of our American Pride, four areas come to mind: Results, respect, re-adjust and rest.

I want to talk to you about results; results come in many different ways. Results are financial, health and spiritual. You have to focus on things that count because it really does all count, but the bottom line, at the end of the day, I'm always asking myself this question, "What have I accomplished today, did it bring me the results that I wanted." That's the question you have to constantly ask yourself and determine what part of the entire pie you're looking at is most important at that particular time. There are times, when I look back at my business ventures, where the price I had to pay for the results were just not worth it; I wish I had those precious moments back; I wish I had the ability to say to my wife, "I love you," more times during the going for that particular result then I did.

The beauty about America and who we are and what we're about – we have the ability to shift, we have the ability to set our "sails" and to re-adjust our "sails" based on how the wind's blowing. See I think there is too many of us, especially in our elected officials, who want to constantly shift the wind, they want to constantly fool with Mother Nature. It's a lot easier just to re-adjust our sails because the wind's going to continually blow in certain directions all the time. Don't curse the wind, don't blame the wind, it's all going to work out if we stay on course.

Adults have to rest, sometimes we're so busy trying to make payroll, or we're so busy trying to be human doers versus human beings that we really can't stop and smell the roses. A good friend said to me, "Randy, you know what you need to do? You need to really stop and slow down because you're so noisy that you cannot hear what God has to say to you." He was one of my mentors, that's one of the guys I have in my corner. So I took my mentor's advice and I slowed down, took a few days off and found the answer I was seeking.

All right, let's round over to our **I** of our American Pride. Two things right up front, very little debate: Individualism and independence. Independence, free thinking is very, very important. We have to think things through more clearly and be intelligent about our choices. There are things that are taking place right now that do not make sense. They're inconsistent, we have to start doing a better job of holding our elected official's feet to the fire. Here's my advice to you – and I'm going to say this again down our American Pride journey – you don't like what you see, elections are coming up; stand up and vote. Be careful, on the intelligence side, understand how your elected officials stand on the issues, if you don't determine what your values are and know your political philosophy beforehand you can be overwhelmed by the media's spin.

If we go back to basic economics and we didn't teach our children why communism failed, why democracy works, they will not be educated. Communism says that the people are too dumb, we're going to take the money away from them and they will serve the state. Democracy doesn't do that. Democracy says the state will serve the people. Now, I know some of you are saying, "Well, we're going in another direction." No we're not. This is America. IT'S OUR CHOICE!

Keep in mind the **I** also stands for, "It's your choice." You've got to be inspired, to be able to get up in the morning and be able to make a difference and make changes. Our elected officials work for who? They work for us, if they don't want to do the job, get them out of office, it's that simple I've seen it, it's the American system, it's the American way, let's get this done together.

Moving over to our **C's** of American Pride and we're almost done. We're rounding 3rd, or almost rounding 3rd. I have lived by the Three C's for a very long time, it has served me well as a young man and serves me well today.

I can remember my father, years ago I was twenty-five years of age I had a good week, for those of you that don't know me, I've been in pay-for-performance compensation package since I was nineteen years of age. I have never had a system where you pay me and I show up. I've always been involved in a system that lets me show you how well I do and then you pay me based on performance. Great system and you make a lot of money that way. Back to dad, I'll never forget this – I happened to have a very good week I met my dad on a Thursday for lunch. Dad said to me, as I was sitting there at the lunch table in my workout gear, "Son, are you not feeling well?" I replied, "No dad, I've had a very good week." He looked at me and asked, "Are your bills paid?" I of course at that age said, "No dad, they're not." He firmly said, "Then do me a favor, get back to your apartment, get your suit and tie on and go back out, beat the streets and go make more calls and make some more sales, go make a difference about four or five more times today."

That was a lesson that has stuck with me for over twenty-five years. This story applies to my Three C's; if we live this, we teach our children this, we're not going to make mistakes. Our elected officials also should live by those rules as well.

The first **C** is character. The second **C** is communications and the third **C** is commitment to excellence. We have to be committed to our nation. I can't believe, once again, that our elected officials on Capitol Hill are even considering some of the legislation that is going to put this country in dire straits.

That's not a commitment toward excellence, they can't sleep at night, I don't buy it. These three C's, I encourage us to live by them and I encourage our elected officials to live by them. As my father asked me, "Does it pass the Three C test?"

Our children, this is what I am so worried about, are the foundation and future of this great country. We want to make sure they get it, because I truly believe if they get the wrong message, they are going to have major problems as they go after their dreams.

It's really amazing to me that our so-called celebrities go to other countries and bow down to leaderships that are against the fiber of America. Yet they've made their fortunes in this country and yet they are constantly bad mouthing America. Here is my advice to them: "Stay over there, give your money to that country – you can't make that much money in Argentina, and in other parts of the world. Let's ship them over there, "New Rules," America's new rules. (Do you think the HBO host that I am referring too will read this part?) We don't have boats rushing to other countries, Americans begging other countries to let us into their country, the boats are from other countries coming here, because it's America, it's called OPPORTUNITY.

I want to cover more of the **C's**. I want to go into number two of the Three C's and that is of course, our citizenship. Don't take it for granted. We have a tremendous immigration problem. We've got to fix this because it is killing our economy. It's killing our healthcare. Citizenship is something that we should not take for granted, this is a prized possession, it's a trophy on our wall that we constantly hold up. Let's protect it.

And let's not forget about our chamber of commerce. Chamber of commerce are the faces of our business community. We have over 7,800 Chamber of commerce throughout the country. We have chambers throughout the world they are called Amchams, American Chamber of Commerce Abroad. Chambers of Commerce are there to promote and protect our business community, it's part of the fiber in the American flag. Here is a brief outline of the chamber world for your information. Chambers are good for business and here is why:

- 1599 first chamber was born in France.
- 1770 first chamber was born in the state of New York to rally the against the Stamp Act.
- 1773 first local chamber was born in Charleston S.C.
- By 1890 more than 40 chambers across the country were gaining strength to Promote and Protect Commerce.
- 1912 the U.S. Chamber was born.
- In the 50 and 60's many chambers focused on job creation and Industrial recruitment.
- Today, According to the ACCE, there are more than 7,800 chambers of commerce.[7]

A chamber of commerce is a voluntary association whose membership is comprised of companies, civic leaders, and individual business people. Its members seek to promote the interests of business, typically in a broad-based way. Chambers of commerce exists on municipal, state, regional, national, and even international levels. Today, chambers of commerce—sometimes called boards of trade or commercial associations—can be found in most of the world's industrialized countries.

In the United States, the first chamber of commerce was created in 1768 in New York City. Its stated objectives encompassed "encouraging commerce, supporting industry, adjusting disputes relative to trade and navigation, and producing such laws and regulations as may be found necessary for the benefit of trade in general." Soon other chambers of commerce formed in other major cities. Arising in quick succession during the 19th century, chambers of commerce spread throughout the land and today number in the thousands.

At the local level, chambers of commerce strive to develop and publicize business opportunities in their communities, as well as work for the betterment of local schools and other community institutions. Local chambers of commerce offer a range of programs and services to their members, including information and advice on timely business matters, opportunities for networking, and a variety of publications. Local chambers of commerce also provide their members with numerous forums—task forces, committees, special events, and so on—in which to express their specific views and concerns, whether pertaining to the challenges facing small businesses or to the issues surrounding international commerce. Depending on their geographic settings, local chambers of commerce can be small or large in terms of their membership and scope of activities.

At the national level, chambers of commerce function as a unified voice for their affiliates. The U.S. Chamber of Commerce, for example, counts individual companies, affiliate chambers of commerce, and trade and professional associations among its members. Through them, it represents more than three million business organizations and individuals. Founded as a national federation in 1912 and headquartered in Washington, D.C., the national chamber was instrumental in persuading the federal government to institute a national budget and in gaining passage of the Federal Reserve Act. Its chief aims are to: stop perceived over regulation; push down business taxes; improve labor relations; increase production, develop new markets; provide more jobs; raise educational levels; build better cities; and keep organized business strong and increasingly effective.

To carry out its mission, the national chamber maintains a large staff that engages in a broad spectrum of activities, ranging from informing and counseling its members on key government developments to conducting policy studies and issuing reports, bulletins, booklets, and periodicals. In addition, the national chamber maintains a vigorous stance in making its policies and member's viewpoints known to federal agency personnel, members of Congress, and other public officials. Augmenting the national chamber are four regional offices and 50 foreign-based American chambers of commerce.

At the global level is the International Chamber of Commerce, founded in 1920. This organization constitutes an international federation of business organizations and individuals and as such serves as a powerful voice for business interests worldwide. It holds the highest-ranking status afforded to organizations the United Nations calls on in a consultative capacity. It also operates a prominent court of arbitration to settle international business disputes; utilizes teams of experts to formulate solutions to problems in such areas as communications, law, and financial relations; and issues a quarterly publication entitled World Trade. Headquartered in Paris, the International Chamber of Commerce functions as a vital mechanism for articulating global business concerns to world opinion leaders and the public at large.

Junior chambers of commerce, known as the Jaycees, also originated in the 1920s. These associations, evolving from the larger chamber of commerce movement, are composed of young business people in their twenties and thirties. Prevalent throughout the United States and in many other countries as well, junior chambers of commerce principally devote their energies to projects of community improvement.

What does a chamber of commerce do? The Chamber improves our community by:

The variety and scope of Chamber activities are unlimited. The Chamber represents and promotes the area's business economy, and encourages business and industrial investment, broadening the tax base and providing employment. To business prospects and newcomers, the Chamber represents the community's pride and self-image.

Chambers of commerce is increasingly involved in non-commercial areas, such as education, human relations, and environmental, cultural and governmental concerns. These challenges have caused Chambers of Commerce to become a viable force in seeking solutions to today's social problems. Chambers of Commerce influence national, state and local legislation affecting business.

- creating jobs
- implementing beautification programs

- improving education
- lobbying local, regional and state government on behalf of our member businesses
- supporting new and existing businesses through our Award-winning BREP Program
- campaigning for improved streets and highways
- stimulating economic industrial, commercial and agricultural growth
- promoting quality of life for the entire community

Joining your local chamber of commerce may just be one of the best moves that you can make for your business. It offers many benefits, many of which are unknown to many business owners.

Moving right along with our American Pride, we're on the 2nd **A** of our American Pride and several things come to mind and it really does bother me. I'm sick of apathy, I don't know about you but, next to apathy this apologetic mentality that for some reason our elected officials are apologizing for what America is, who we are and what we're about. We don't have to apologize, for being Americans! Who started that movement? We are who we are. We're the greatest nation that there is, the apologetic attitude that we have among some of our elected officials has got to stop! Write the letters, tell them how you feel, this is America, we're the best. I'm going to read you something that I ran across. It is good timing for what this all about.

There was an elderly gentlemen, Eight-Three years of age that arrived in Paris by plane at the French customs. It took a few minutes to locate his passport in his carry on. "You have been to

France before, monsieur?" The customs officer, asked sarcastically. The gentleman admitted that he had been to France previously. "Then you should know enough to have your passport ready."

The American said, "The last time I was here, I didn't have to show it." "Impossible! Americans have to show their passport on arrival in France." The American senior gave the Frenchman a long, hard look. Then he quietly explained, "Well young man, when I came ashore at Omaha Beach on D-Day in 1944 to help liberate this country, I couldn't find a single Frenchman to show my passport to." No apologies whatsoever.

Let's talk about access of information in the **A**, of our American Pride; what is being presented to us? We have this mind numbing media that controls a lot of people's ability to think. All the information on the internet we are exposed to can take over our minds so we do not fully understand what we are being presented with.

It was funny. One night, I had two network TV channels on at the same time. It was a split screen. The two were national news channels hosting the doom and gloom fest, it's amazing to me, if I was from another country, or I was a child or I was just plain stupid, there would be a lot of confusion about who's right and who's wrong. You have ranting, raving; you have this person's number one, that person's number one. So it does get confusing with the amount of information that we have to process. Make sure we have correct information. Believe me, it's out there. Voting records of our elected officials are out there. You have to know, though, where you stand on our economic policy and what you believe drives America.

We're going to round this off to the end of our American Pride and we are almost finished, the **N** - our nation is noble. And NOW! Do something NOW. Make a difference NOW. Don't wait until tomorrow. Discipline weighs ounces, regret weighs tons. Stand up for what you believe in and take charge and do it NOW! If not for you, do it for your children and your grandchildren.

I'm a small business owner, I'm no one special, I've grinded, I'm the guy that constantly digs the ditch and just keeps going, I pay attention, I have stick-a-tivity. I don't jump from job to job, I don't sit there and look at other companies to start something here and move over to there, I endure and it's very, very important to be able to do this. But more importantly, I'm able to do this because I'm in America.

That's the important part and that's the message I want to make sure you hear. It is about motivation, it is about fun, it's about meaning and it is about inspiration.

I saw a movie the other night and it was called "Conversations with God," apparently, it's a true story, I believe that it is also a best-selling book, but what's interesting about this movie – the two actors are on the bus and, the actor says to the other actor, "Goodbye." she says, "No, it's not goodbye, it's I'll see you later." Because goodbye is really a definite ending.

I will see you later because we're Americans. We have a commonality an esprit de corps. We want to do the right things that keep this great country on the path of prosperity and, more importantly, the freedom that we enjoy every single day.

Mark Twain said it very well, "Cast the bow lines off of the harbor. Push away from the safety of the shore. Raise your sails. Dream, explore; catch these trade winds."

Go find what America has to offer because, you know, it's out there. All you've got to do is look. All you have to do is appreciate sometimes what's in front of you.

Here is the **PRIDE** that you've been waiting for, American Pride very little debate, no discussion, pretty straight forward. The pride stands for **People Require Individual Democracy Everywhere**! Remember-

IT's OUR Country IT's **<u>YOUR</u>** Choice!

American Pride: By and for our Young Americans – It's their Country Too, Soon it Will be Their Choice.

Part Two – Young Americans

"Children are the world's most valuable resource
and its best hope for the future."
—John F. Kennedy, 35th President of the United States

I want to welcome you to Part two of this chapter on how the American Pride series for our young Americans came to fruition, along with some funny lessons and experiences that I dealt with putting this series together for our young Americans. My first series was produced for American adults as you have read. I present this and other lectures around the country. They are fun energetic and very thought provoking. I decided to produce the 3rd series: **A.m.e.r.i.c.a.n. P.r.i.d.e.** **By** *and for our young* **Americans**, because our children are truly the future of this great county. I believe that the great American legacy of freedom, democracy and all the great things that our country was founded on will soon be in the hands of our children. It has to be the right message! They have to get it! As the subtitle states; "It's Their Country Too and Soon it Will be Their Choice."

To accomplish this presentation, we teamed up with the students and faculty of the Freedom Academy in Scottsdale Arizona. I visited the school to gather the information to produce our 3rd PRIDE series. I don't think that it could have gotten any better than this, well maybe, I am sure that if I found Democracy University it might have trumped our Freedom Academy, it didn't.

Off to the school I went. The homework assignment was given to the entire student body. Grades 1st thru the 8th were asked to do one or two paragraphs on each of the three questions which the principal Linda Hoffman and I decided upon:

1. **What America means to them.**
2. **What they want America to look like in the future.**
3. **What do they feel America will look like in the future based on our current path?**

As you have read previously American Pride is an ACRONYM of meaning and thought and inspiration. I normally create three meanings and inspiration for each letter in American and Pride. I decided to let the students choose their own two or three meanings for each letter.

We had a winner's circle to announce the best of the students' writings. We chose one winner from each grade from the three questions of AMERICAN PRIDE.

I have to tell you a funny story. When I had all of the essays, 300 to be exact and the drawings that went along with the essay from the students, you can see all of this: www.amerianpridee-book.com and please turn your speakers up.

I wanted to hire a student that could assist me with the layout of the book. So after several interviews, I was referred to Jennifer. Her mother and Jennifer met me at my local Starbucks to review the project and tell me what she thought Jennifer could accomplish. After about thirty minutes of Jennifer letting me know how good she was at this type of development (by the way, she was Sixteen at the time) I said ok! Tell me how many hours this will take you and what are your fees per hour? I had a figure around $10 per hour. She very confidently said "$15 per hour." She explained why she was charging almost double the minimum wage for a sixteen year old, I said ok let's go to work.

The funny part of the story is this: The Starbucks manager overheard our negotiations and was very unhappy. She said "$15 per hour?" That's more than I make and she is only sixteen!" Without even thinking, out it came, my free enterprise speech, "Hey, work for someone else they tell you what you are worth, work for yourself and you determine your worth." By the way, Jennifer was worth every dime that was paid to her. She has a very bright future in front of her.

I wanted to include part of the student's writings and what we found as the three to four common concerns of the students in each grade. This will amaze you that 4th graders are starting to use the word "socialism". This is why in one of the chapters I have defined certain words so we know exactly what the word means.

 Before I get to the students, I want to relate a story. I have added the "Ten things you can do to make a difference in America." It was put together in a coffee shop in Northern Arizona, I was there to speak at a chamber of commerce function. My mind was in over - drive that morning! I was in the "Zone" as they say.

Certain members of the Arizona Republican party were involved with the activity that surrounded the American Pride event. The party chair saw the Ten things "you can do" piece and said; "You have to get rid of number one! It's too much like what Obama says all the time, or he says something like that." I sat back, thought about what he said, and decided no, this is good stuff, number one stays! I told the chairman," I don't care who it sounds like, our young Americans need to hear the message of what number one means." "I further explained that this was not a partisan piece, this was about America, and our future." That was a lot of fun saying no and not caving in to what they wanted. I am sure they ripped up my republican ticket! LOL!

"You are the future"
10 things you can do to make a difference in America everyday!

1. Yes you can! @ Whatever you want to do

2. Work hard on yourself - so you can help others

3. Dream BIG - if you don't you will never know!

4. Stay in school - learn and understand

5. Become rich in knowledge

6. NEVER-NEVER GIVE UP!

7. Remember your 3C's - they will serve you well
your entire life!

8. Be a person of caring - for all

9. Love and respect your parents - those who teach you
and those who are around you.
Someone is trying to tell you something.
There is always a message!

10. Put God in your life - he will never leave you!

Always remember - you are special!
There ARE things waiting for you to show up!

The winning essays with the common concerns of our Young Americans from grade 1st through 8th.

1ST GRADE -WINNING ESSAY

Common Concerns:
- Freedom to be and do whatever you want in America
- Follow Laws
- Fair
- God

1st grade winner's essay

"What America means to me is I can be treated fair, and to be free and to follow god and be treated equal"

It is apparent that even the first graders of our society are concerned for their freedom and their rights. They want to follow laws and they want fair and just laws. They also do not want to see God taken out of everyday life.

2ND GRADE AND WINNING ESSAY

Common Concerns:
- Freedom
- Love
- Joy
- Peace

2nd grade winner's essay

"I love America so much, I am so blessed to live in America"

It is obvious that even the second graders love their country and want peace and happiness. They want to have freedom to do what they want.

3RD GRADE AND WINNING ESSAY

Common Concerns:

- Environment
- Freedom
- Love for America
- Less war
- Peace-America loves peace
- More jobs- less debt
- Everyone has a home

3rd grade winner's essay

"What America looks like in the future? People will be nice to each other, people won't steal from each other. People will help each other. America will have freedom. All 50 states will have homes. Everywhere will have green grass and the air won't be polluted. People will walk instead of using cars. People will recycle more. People will have jobs and money. Teachers will have money for supplies."

We can see that even the normal third grader is already worried about having a job, debt and a house in their future. They are concerned about the environment and want peace in the world.

4TH GRADE AND WINNING ESSAY

Common Concerns:

- Freedom
- Stop war
- Honor veterans
- Love and prayer

- Parents staying together
- Helping homeless
- Freedom of religion
- Environment
- Economy
- Stop Terrorism

4th grade winner's essay

"America is an awesome place to live! I like it because it has freedom, brave hero's and honor. without brave hero's to help win wars we would have no freedom. I am proud to be an American I am also proud of our free religion and fair rules. America is the best country ever! I want to change the way people treat the homeless. I also want a better economy, like more jobs that pay more money. they should keep families together by donating money to poor families. that's what I think we should change."

It is clear that even though these kids are in 4th grade, they are concerned for their future freedom of religion, economy, and terrorism. They want to help people in need and keep the environment safe and healthy.

5TH GRADE AND WINNING ESSAY

Common Concerns:
- Peace-no more war
- No more debt-job shortages-better economy
- Love America for freedom
- Concerned about terrorism-security
- Environment-solar power

- Flying cars
- Freedom of religion

5th grade winner's essay

"America is a free land and i am amazingly grateful for that. this world could be and will be in the future very dangerous or safe and free from evil. we are still standing and no person is ruling us and we do what we please. what do you feel about America and what do you think should be changed? America has protectors, people in the army and i am pretty sure we have cameras for terrorist protection. to be hones I think this earth is going slowly to the ground and right now IT'S hovering. I don't know why our economy is bad and i do know people are trying to help America. i bet on 20% of earth will be nature in about 300 years maybe. at least in the end most join god and life will be unimaginable. i honor those who fight and fought for our lives and America. crazy people destroyed to twin towers on this day and caused people to jump out. I want to get rid of these useless factories and buildings that kill nature. it's wrong to add any more. I also wish in the future we discover a way to stop earthquakes, hurricanes, tornadoes and volcanoes. i don't want robots invited because i know that they turn bad in movies. I want piece in America and everywhere in the world."

It is obvious that the children in today's society are much more aware than we give them credit for. They are concerned about their future life and about the future of our declining economy. They want to stop war and they hope for a better future than is in the distance right now.

6TH GRADE AND WINNING ESSAY

Common Concerns:

- Love of America
- Economy-debt
- Freedom of Religion
- Environment
- Worry about America
- Worry about economy

6th Grade Winner's essay

"What does America mean to you? Is a very heart-bound question with so many answers that all revolve around your opinion. To me, however, America is more than a place that God put on the globe, it's a home and more importantly it's my home. Many call it the land of the free and the home of the brave. I call it that and a lot more! All of the men and women putting their life on the line in Iraq probably don't want to but do they? Yes! Why? Because they are like me and they love America and are willing to die to protect it. I, myself am planning to join the USAF. My dad was in the air force and his dad was in the air force and his dad was too, so was his whole generations of moms. I bet they didn't like it, but they showed they loved America so much by staying in and not quitting the moment it got hard. Sure America isn't perfect, it has its up and downs but all new immigrants call it heaven, all of the illegal immigrants dig under the boarder because they heard that they can be free and be treated well and fairly. That just goes to show how good our government is and how fortunate we are that we don't have to run away from it to be treated well. I personally, don't think that people take that seriously enough.

I bet this made you wake up and think "WOW I didn't realize how important this is!" and I hope you do, because this is what America means to me."

It is clear that these 6th graders want to make a difference in the world through keeping people loyal to their country or merely helping the environment. This generation of kids is the future of our country.

7TH GRADE AND WINNING ESSAY

Common Concerns:
- Freedom of choice
- More schools
- Less pollution

7th grade Winner's Essay

"Do you want to know what America means to me? America means to me freedom and love. I think that because it is free here. America gives you the freedom to make you own choices. I want to thank the men and women who fight for our freedom."

These 7th graders want to be able to make their own decisions in the future and they want to keep education present in everyday life. They are also concerned for our environment.

8TH GRADE AND WINNING ESSAY

Common Concerns:
- Freedom to say and be anything
- Socialism
- Economy
- Healthcare

8th grade winner's essay

"America is the greatest nation on earth. The words that come to mind when I think of America are freedom, greatness and liberty. I think of the hundreds of thousands of men and women who have sacrificed their lives so we can enjoy the freedoms we do today. America has aided many other countries in the past, but now I fear America is the country in need of help. Our beloved nation has fallen into a terrible rut. America's constitution and very freedom is being threatened by an out of control government. Every day there are new laws and regulations being passed and American people are watching as there rights are being ripped away. I worry and hope not, but I see America on a deadly path to socialism which is undoubtedly a road to communism. America's freedom depends on getting back to a little thing called the constitution, or our nation is doomed. We must drop the political correctness and greed and pay attention to what's going on in Washington or we are doomed, it's common sense."

We can see that these are very insightful 8th graders and they are extremely aware of what Congress is doing at the present time. They are at the age when they are thinking about their future and they want to make a difference to make the country they live in and love a better place.

In conclusion, we can see that the youth of America is very insightful to what is happening in America. Every child, 1st through 8th grade, seems to want the same things: Freedom of religion, freedom to be anything and say anything, a renewed environment, and for peace in the country. Adults sometimes believe that kids don't really understand what is going on and they have no stresses, however, it is just the opposite. Even the first graders are worried about not being able to have God in their daily life and they worry that they will not have freedom as they get older. These kids deserve credit for their knowledge because they are the future of America.

I want to finish this chapter with this speech that was emailed to me as I was writing this book. I feel that it ties into this chapter very nicely.

A Speech Every American High School Principal Should Give –

By Dennis Prager

Tuesday, July 13, 2010

To the students and faculty of our high school:

I am your new principal, and honored to be so. There is no greater calling than to teach young people.

I would like to apprise you of some important changes coming to our school. I am making these changes because I am convinced that most of the ideas that have dominated public education in America have worked against you, against your teachers and against our country.

First, this school will no longer honor race or ethnicity. I could not care less if your racial makeup is black, brown, red, yellow or white. I could not care less if your origins are African, Latin American, Asian or European, or if your ancestors arrived here on the Mayflower or on slave ships.

The only identity I care about, the only one this school will recognize, is your individual identity -- your character, your scholarship, your humanity. And the only national identity this school will care about is American. This is an American public school, and American public schools were created to make better Americans.

If you wish to affirm an ethnic, racial or religious identity through school, you will have to go elsewhere. We will end all ethnicity-, race- and non-American nationality-based celebrations. They undermine the motto of America, one of its three central values -- e pluribus unum, "from many, one." And this school will be guided by America's values.

This includes all after-school clubs. I will not authorize clubs that divide students based on any identities. This includes race, language, religion, sexual orientation or whatever else may become in vogue in a society divided by political correctness.

Your clubs will be based on interests and passions, not blood, ethnic, racial or other physically defined ties. Those clubs just cultivate narcissism -- an unhealthy preoccupation with the self -- while the purpose of education is to get you to think beyond yourself. So we will have clubs that transport you to the wonders and glories of art, music, astronomy, languages you do not already speak, carpentry and more. If the only extracurricular activities you can imagine being interesting in are those based on ethnic, racial or sexual identity, that means that little outside of yourself really interests you.

Second, I am uninterested in whether English is your native language. My only interest in terms of language is that you leave this school speaking and writing English as fluently as possible. The English language has united America's citizens for over 200 years, and it will unite us at this school. It is one of the indispensable reasons this country of immigrants has always come to be one country. And if you leave this school without excellent English language skills, I would be remiss in my duty to ensure that you will be prepared to successfully compete in the American job market. We will learn other languages here -- it is deplorable that most Americans only speak English -- but if you want classes taught in your native language rather than in English, this is not your school.

Third, because I regard learning as a sacred endeavor, everything in this school will reflect learning's elevated status. This means, among other things, that you and your teachers will dress accordingly. Many people in our society dress more formally for Hollywood events than for church or school. These people have their priorities backward. Therefore, there will be a formal dress code at this school.

Fourth, no obscene language will be tolerated anywhere on this school's property -- whether in class, in the hallways or at athletic events. If you can't speak without using the f-word, you can't speak. By obscene language I mean the words banned by the Federal Communications Commission, plus epithets such as "Nigger," even when used by one black student to address another black, or "bitch," even when addressed by a girl to a girlfriend. It is my intent that by the time you leave this school, you will be among the few your age to instinctively distinguish between the elevated and the degraded, the holy and the obscene.

Fifth, we will end all self-esteem programs. In this school, self-esteem will be attained in only one way -- the way people attained it until decided otherwise a generation ago -- by earning it. One immediate consequence is that there will be one valedictorian, not eight.

Sixth, and last, I am reorienting the school toward academics and away from politics and propaganda. No more time will devoted to scaring you about smoking and caffeine, or terrifying you about sexual harassment or global warming. No more semesters will be devoted to condom wearing and teaching you to regard sexual relations as only or primarily a health issue. There will be no more attempts to convince you that you are a victim because you are not white, or not male, or not heterosexual or not Christian. We will have failed if any one of you graduates this school and does not consider him or her inordinately lucky -- to be alive and to be an American.

Now, please stand and join me in the Pledge of Allegiance to the flag of our country. As many of you do not know the words, your teachers will hand them out to you.

SOON IT WILL BE THEIR CHOICE!

Chapter 6

Thirteen Most Patriotic Speeches in American History

"Communication is the real work of leadership."
—Nitin Nohria

If one wants to become an effective communicator and also an effective leader for positive change, they must first understand what those qualities entail: In order to achieve them, one must study, observe and learn from those who have already obtained these attributes.

Patriotism can be defined as "Love of and Devotion to One's Country." An effective speech is "The Act of Describing Thoughts, Feelings and Perceptions in Words." Characteristics of a great leader include: **High Energy Level, Goal Oriented Behavior, Self-Confidence, Creativity, Clear Vision, and Commitment to Excellence, Strong Integrity, Being an Agent of Change and Being a Positive Role Model.**

One who delivers a great patriotic speech will have a love of country, a clear vision of what he/she wants to accomplish and the ability to lead and motivate others to follow him/her in order to achieve this vision.

In order to be on this list of great American patriotic speeches, the speech needs to:

Be Memorable and Quotable
Contain a Clear Vision of the Future
Contain Clear Objective Goals
Achieve the Goals Laid Out in the Speech
Be Delivered in a Strong Effective Manner
Create a Lasting Positive Change in America

These Top Thirteen Patriotic Speeches in American History have lifted hearts in dark times, gave hope in despair, refined the characters of men, inspired brave feats, gave courage to the weary, honored the dead and, most importantly, changed the course of history.

Farewell Address to the Nation – Ronald Reagan

January 11, 1989

Before I say my formal good-bye, maybe I should tell you what I'm up to now that I'm out of office. Well, I'm still giving speeches, still sounding off about those things I didn't get accomplished while I was president.

High on my agenda are three things. First, I'm out there stumping to help future presidents – Republican or Democrat – get those tools they need to bring the budget under control. And those tools are a line-item veto and a constitutional amendment to balance the budget. Second, I'm out there talking up the need to do something about political gerrymandering. This is the practice of rigging the boundaries of congressional districts. It is the greatest single blot on the integrity of our nation's electoral system, and it's high time we did something about it. And third, I'm talking up the idea of repealing the Twenty-second Amendment, to the Constitution, the amendment that prevents a president from serving more than two terms. I believe it's a preemption of the people's right to vote for whomever they want as many times as they want.

So I'm back where I came in – out there on the mashed potato circuit. I have a feeling I'll be giving speeches until I'm called to the great beyond and maybe even after. All it will take is for St. Peter to say, "Ronald Wilson Reagan, what do you have to say for yourself? Speak up."

"Well, sir, unaccustomed as I am . . ."

My fellow Americans:

This is the thirty-fourth time I'll speak to you from the Oval Office and the last. We've been together for eight years now, and soon it'll be time for me to go. But before I do, I wanted to share some thoughts, some of which I've been saying for a long time.

It's been the honor of my life to be your president. So many of you have written the past few weeks to say thanks, but I could say as much to you. Nancy and I are grateful for the opportunity you gave us to serve.

One of the things about the presidency is that you're always somewhat apart. You spend a lot of time going by too fast in a car someone else is driving, and seeing the people through tinted glass – the parents holding up a child, and the wave you saw too late and couldn't return. And so many times I wanted to stop and reach out from behind the glass, and connect. Well, maybe I can do a little of that tonight.

People ask how I feel about leaving. And the fact is, "parting is such sweet sorrow." The sweet part is California, and the ranch and freedom. The sorrow – the good-byes, of course, and leaving this beautiful place.

You know, down the hall and up the stairs from this office is the part of the White House where the presidents and his family live. There are a few favorite windows I have up there that I like to stand and look out of early in the morning. The view is over the grounds here to the Washington Monument, and then the Mall and the Jefferson Memorial. But on mornings when the humidity is low, you can see past the Jefferson to the river, the Potomac, and the Virginia shore. Someone said that's the view Lincoln had when he saw the smoke rising from the Battle of Bull Run. I see more prosaic things: the grass on the banks, the morning traffic as people mark their way to work, now and then a sailboat on the river.

I've been thinking a bit at that window. I've been reflecting on what the past eight years have meant and mean. And the image that comes to mind like a refrain is a nautical one – a small story about a big ship, and a refugee and a sailor. It was back in the early eighties, at the height of the boat people. And the sailor was hard at work on the carrier Midway, which was patrolling the South China Sea. The sailor, like most American servicemen, was young, smart, and fiercely observant. The crew spied on the horizon a leaky little boat. And crammed inside were refugees from Indochina hoping to get to America. The Midway sent a small launch to bring them to the ship and safety. As the refugees made their way through the choppy seas, one spied the sailor on deck and stood up and called out to him. He yelled, "Hello, American sailor. Hello, freedom man."

A small moment with a big meaning, a moment the sailor, who wrote it in a letter, couldn't get out of his mind. And when I saw it, neither could I. Because that's what it was to be an American in the 1980s. We stood, again, for freedom. I know we always have, but in the past few years the world again, and in a way, we ourselves – rediscovered it.

It's been quite a journey this decade, and we held together through some stormy seas. And at the end, together, we are reaching our destination.

The fact is, from Grenada to the Washington and Moscow summits, from the recession of '81 to '82, to the expansion that began in late '82 and continues to this day, we've made a difference. The way I see it, there were two great triumphs, two things that I'm proudest of. One is the economic recovery, in which the people of America created – and filled – 19 million new jobs. The other is the recovery of our morale. America is respected again in the world and looked to for leadership.

Something that happened to me a few years ago reflects some of this. It was back in 1981, and I was attending my first big economic summit, which was held that year in Canada. The meeting place rotates among the member countries. The opening meeting was a formal dinner for the heads of government of the seven industrialized nations. Now, I sat there like the new kid in school and listened, and it was all the Francois this and Helmut that. They dropped titles and spoke to one another on a first-name basis. Well, at one point I sort of learned in an said, "My name's Ron." Well, in that same year, we began the actions we felt would ignite an economic comeback – cut taxes and regulation, started to cut spending. And soon the recovery began.

Two years later another economic summit, with pretty much the same cast. At the big opening meeting we all got together, and all of a sudden, just for a moment, I saw that everyone was just sitting there looking at me. And then one of them broke the silence. "Tell us about the American miracle," he said.

Well, back in 1980, when I was running for president, it was all so different. Some pundits said our programs would result in catastrophe. Our views on foreign affairs would cause war. Our plans for the economy would cause inflation to soar and bring about economic collapse. I even remember one highly respected economist saying, back in 1982, that "the engines of economic growth have shut down here, and they're likely to stay that way for years to come." Well, he and the other opinion leaders were wrong. The fact is, what they called "radical" was really "right". What they called "dangerous" was just "desperately needed."

And in all of that time I won a nickname, "The Great Communicator." But I never thought it was my style or the words I used that made a difference: It was the content. I wasn't a great communicator, but I communicated great things, and they didn't spring full bloom from my brow, they came from the heart of a great nation – from our experience, our wisdom, and our belief in the principles that have guided us for two centuries. They called it the Reagan revolution. Well, I'll accept that, but for me it always seemed more like the great rediscovery, a rediscover of our values and our common sense.

Common sense told us that when you put a big tax on something, the people will produce less of it. So, we cut the people's tax rates, and the people produced more than ever before. The economy bloomed like a plant that had been cut back and could not grow quicker and stronger. Our economic program brought about the longest peacetime expansion in our history: real family income up, the poverty rate down, entrepreneurship booming, and an explosion in research and new technology. We're exporting more than ever because American industry became more competitive and at the same time, we summoned the national will to knock down protectionist walls abroad instead of erecting them at home. Common sense also told us that to preserve the peace, we'd have to become strong again after years of weakness and confusion. So, we rebuilt our defenses, and this New Year we toasted the new peacefulness around the globe. Not only have the superpowers actually begun to reduce their stockpiles of nuclear weapons – and hope for even more progress is bright – but the regional conflicts that rack the globe are also beginning to cease. The Persian Gulf is no longer a war zone. The Soviets are leaving Afghanistan. The Vietnamese are preparing to pull out of Cambodia, and an American-mediated accord will soon send 50,000 Cuban troops home to Angola.

The lesson of all this was, of course, that because we're a great nation, our challenges seem complex. It will always be this way. But as long as we remember our first principles and believe in ourselves, the future will always be ours. And something else we learned: Once you begin a great movement, there's no telling where it will end. We meant to change a nation, and instead, we changed a world.

Countries across the globe are turning to free markets and free speech and turning away from the ideologies of the past. For them, the great rediscovery of the 1980s has been that, lo and behold, the moral way of government is the practical way of government: Democracy, the profoundly good, is also profoundly productive.

When you've got to the point when you can celebrate the anniversaries of your thirty-ninth birthday, you can sit back sometimes, review your life, and see it flowing before you. For me there was a fork in the river, and it was right in the middle of my life. I never meant to go into politics. It wasn't my intention when I was young. But I was raised to believe you had to pay your way for the blessings bestowed on you. I was happy with my career in the entertainment world, but I ultimately went into politics because I wanted to protect something precious.

Ours was the first revolution in the history of mankind that truly reversed the course of government, and with three little words: "We the people." "We the people" tell the government what to do, it doesn't tell us. "We the people" are the driver, the government is the car. And we decide where it should go, and by what route, and how fast. Almost all the world's constitutions are documents in which governments tell the people what their privileges are. Our Constitution is a document in which "We the people" tell the government what it is allowed to do. "We the people" are fee. This belief has been the underlying basis for everything I've tried to do these past eight years.

But back in the 1960s, when I began, it seemed to me that we'd begun reversing the order of things – that through more and more rules and regulations and confiscatory taxes, the government was taking more of our money, more of our options, and more of our freedom. I went into politics in part to put up my hand and say, "Stop." I was a citizen politician, and it seemed the right thing for a citizen to do.

I think we have stopped a lot of what needed stopping. And I hope we have once again reminded the people that man is not free unless government is limited. There's a clear cause and effect here that is as neat and predictable as a law of physics: As government expands, liberty contracts.

Nothing is less free than pure communism, and yet we have, the past few years, forged a satisfying new closeness with the Soviet Union. I've been asked if this isn't a gamble, and my answer is no because we're basing our actions not on words but deeds. The détente of the 1970s was based not on actions but promises. They'd promise to treat their own people and the people of the world better. But the gulag was still the gulag, and the state was still expansionist, and they still waged proxy wars in Africa, Asia, and Latin America.

Well, this time, so far, it's different. President Gorbachev has brought about some internal democratic reforms and begun the withdrawal from Afghanistan. He has also freed prisoners whose names I've given him every time we've met.

But life has a way of reminding you of big things through small incidents. Once, during the heady days of the Moscow summit, Nancy and I decided to break off from the entourage one afternoon to visit the shops on Arbat Street – that's a little street just off Moscow's main shopping area. Even though our visit was a surprise, every Russian there immediately recognized us and called out our names and reached for our hands. We were just about swept away by the warmth. You could almost feel the possibilities in all that joy. But within seconds, a KGB detail pushed their way toward us and began pushing and shoving the people in the crowd. It was an interesting moments. It reminded me that while the man of the street in the Soviet Union yearns for peace, the government is Communist. And those who run it are Communists, and that means we and they view such issues as freedom and human rights very differently.

We must keep up our guard, but we must also continue to work together to lessen and eliminate tension and mistrust. My view is that President Gorbachev is different from previous Soviet leaders. I think he knows some of the things wrong with his society and is trying to fix them. We wish him well. And we'll continue to work to make sure that the Soviet Union that eventually emerges from this process is a less threatening one. What it all boils down to is this. I want the new closeness to continue. And it will, as long as we make it clear that we will continue to act in a certain way as long as they continue to act in a helpful manner. If and when they don't, at first pull your punches. If they persist, pull the plug. It's still trust but verify. It's still play, but cut the cards. It's still watch closely. And don't be afraid to see what you see.

I've been asked if I have any regrets. Well, I do. The deficit is one. I've been talking a great deal about that lately, but tonight isn't for arguments. And I'm going to hold my tongue. But an observation: I've had my share of victories in the Congress, but what few people noticed is that I never won anything you didn't win for me. They never saw my troops, they never saw Reagan's regiments, the American people. You won every battle with every call you made and letter you wrote demanding action. Well, action is still needed. If we're to finish the job, Reagan's regiments will have to become the Bush brigades. Soon he'll be the chief, and he'll need you every bit as much as I did.

Finally, there is a great tradition of warnings in presidential farewells, and I've got one that's been on my mind for some time.

THIRTEEN MOST PATRIOTIC SPEECHES IN AMERICAN HISTORY   97

But oddly enough it starts with one of the things I'm proudest of in the past eight years: the resurgence of national pride that I called the new patriotism. This national feeling is good, but it won't count for much, and it won't last unless it's grounded in thoughtfulness and knowledge.

An informed patriotism is what we want. And are we doing a good enough job teaching our children what America is and what she represents in the long history of the world? Those of us who are over thirty-five or so years of age grew up in a different America. We were taught, very directly, what it means to be an American. And we absorbed, almost in the air, a love of country and an appreciation of its institutions. If you didn't get these things from your family, you got them from the neighborhood, from the father down the street who fought in Korea of the family who lost someone at Anzio. Or you could get a sense of patriotism from school. And if all else failed, you could get a sense of patriotism from the popular culture. The movies celebrated democratic values and implicitly reinforced the idea that America was special. TV was like that, too, through the mid-sixties.

But now, we're about to enter the nineties, and some things have changed. Younger parents aren't sure that an unambivalent appreciation of America is the right thing to teach modern children. And as for those who create the popular culture, well-grounded patriotism is no longer the style. Our spirit is back, but we haven't reinstitutionalized it. We've got to do a better job of getting across that America is freedom – freedom of speech, freedom of religion, freedom of enterprise. And freedom is special and rate. It's fragile; it needs production [protection].

So, we've got to teach history based not on what's in fashion but what's important: Why the Pilgrims came here, who Jimmy Doolittle was, and what those thirty seconds over Tokyo meant.

You know, four years ago on the fortieth anniversary of D day, I read a letter from a young woman writing of her late father, who'd fought on Omaha Beach. Her name was Lisa Zanatta Henn, and she said, "We will always remember, we will never forget what the boys of Normandy did." Well, let's help her keep her word. If we forget what we did, we won't know who we are. I'm warning of an eradication of the American memory that could result, ultimately, in an erosion of the American spirit. Let's start with some basics: more attention to American history and a greater emphasis on civic ritual. And let me offer lesson number one about America: All great change in America begins at the dinner table. So, tomorrow night in the kitchen I hope the talking begins. And children, if your parents haven't been teaching you what it means to be an American, let 'em know and nail 'em on it. That would be a very American thing to do.

And that's about all I have to say tonight. Except for one thing. The past few days when I've been at that window upstairs, I've thought a bit of the "shining city upon a hill." The phrase comes from John Winthrop, who wrote it to describe the America he imagined. What he imagined was important because he was an early Pilgrim, an early freedom man. He journeyed here on what today we'd call a little wooden boat; and like the other Pilgrims, he was looking for a home that would be free.

I've spoken of the shining city all my political life, but I don't know if I ever quite communicated what I saw when I said it. But in my mind it was a tall proud city built on rocks stronger than oceans, wind-swept, God-blessed, and teeming with people of all kinds living in harmony and peace, a city with free ports that hummed with commerce and creativity, and if there had to be city walls, the walls had doors and the doors were open to anyone with the will and the heart to get here. That's how I saw it, and see it still.

And how stand the city on this winter night? More prosperous, more secure, and happier than it was eight years ago. But more than that; after two hundred years, two centuries, she still stands strong and true on the granite ridge, and her glow has held steady no matter what storm. And she's still a beacon, still a magnet for all who must have freedom, for all the pilgrims from all the lost places who are hurtling through the darkness, toward home.

We've done our part. And as I walk off into the city streets, a final word to the men and women of the Reagan revolution, the men and women across America who for eight years did the work that brought America back. My friends: We did it. We weren't just marking time. We made a difference. We made the city stronger. We made the city freer, and we left her in good hands. All in all, not bad, not bad at all.

And so, good-bye, God bless you, and God bless the United States of America.

"I Have a Dream" by Dr. Martin Luther King

August 23, 1963

I am happy to join with you today in what will go down in history as the greatest demonstration for freedom in the history of our nation.

Five score years ago, a great American, in whose symbolic shadow we stand today, signed the Emancipation Proclamation. This momentous decree came as a great beacon light of hope to millions of Negro slaves who had been seared in the flames of withering injustice. It came as a joyous daybreak to end the long night of their captivity.

But one hundred years later, the Negro still is not free. One hundred years later, the life of the Negro is still sadly crippled by the manacles of segregation and the chains of discrimination. One hundred years later, the Negro lives on a lonely island of poverty in the midst of a vast ocean of material prosperity. One hundred years later, the Negro is still languished in the corners of American society and finds himself an exile in his own land. And so we've come here today to dramatize a shameful condition.

In a sense we've come to our nation's capital to cash a check. When the architects of our republic wrote the magnificent words of the Constitution and the Declaration of Independence, they were signing a promissory note to which every American was to fall heir. This note was a promise that all men, yes, black men as well as white men, would be guaranteed the "unalienable Rights" of "Life, Liberty and the pursuit of Happiness." It is obvious today that America has defaulted on this promissory note, insofar as her citizens of color are concerned. Instead of honoring this sacred obligation, America has given the Negro people a bad check, a check which has come back marked "insufficient funds."

But we refuse to believe that the bank of justice is bankrupt.

We refuse to believe that there are insufficient funds in the great vaults of opportunity of this nation. And so, we've come to cash this check, a check that will give us upon demand the riches of freedom and the security of justice.

We have also come to this hallowed spot to remind America of the fierce urgency of Now. This is no time to engage in the luxury of cooling off or to take the tranquilizing drug of gradualism. Now is the time to make real the promises of democracy. Now is the time to rise from the dark and desolate valley of segregation to the sunlit path of racial justice. Now is the time to lift our nation from the quick sands of racial injustice to the solid rock of brotherhood. Now is the time to make justice a reality for all of God's children.

It would be fatal for the nation to overlook the urgency of the moment. This sweltering summer of the Negro's legitimate discontent will not pass until there is an invigorating autumn of freedom and equality. Nineteen sixty-three is not an end, but a beginning. And those who hope that the Negro needed to blow off steam and will now be content will have a rude awakening if the nation returns to business as usual. And there will be neither rest nor tranquility in America until the Negro is granted his citizenship rights. The whirlwinds of revolt will continue to shake the foundations of our nation until the bright day of justice emerges.

But there is something that I must say to my people, who stand on the warm threshold which leads into the palace of justice: In the process of gaining our rightful place, we must not be guilty of wrongful deeds. Let us not seek to satisfy our thirst for freedom by drinking from the cup of bitterness and hatred. We must forever conduct our struggle on the high plane of dignity and discipline. We must not allow our creative protest to degenerate into physical violence. Again and again, we must rise to the majestic heights of meeting physical force with soul force.

The marvelous new militancy which has engulfed the Negro community must not lead us to a distrust of all white people, for many of our white brothers, as evidenced by their presence here today, have come to realize that their destiny is tied up with our destiny. And they have come to realize that their freedom is inextricably bound to our freedom.

We cannot walk alone.

And as we walk, we must make the pledge that we shall always march ahead.

We cannot turn back.

There are those who are asking the devotees of civil rights, "When will you be satisfied?" We can never be satisfied as long as the Negro is the victim of the unspeakable horrors of police brutality. We can never be satisfied as long as our bodies, heavy with the fatigue of travel, cannot gain lodging in the motels of the highways and the hotels of the cities. We cannot be satisfied as long as the Negro's basic mobility is from a smaller ghetto to a larger one. We can never be satisfied as long as our children are stripped of their self-hood and robbed of their dignity by a sign stating: "For Whites Only." We cannot be satisfied as long as a Negro in Mississippi cannot vote and a Negro in New York believes he has nothing for which to vote. No, no, we are not satisfied, and we will not be satisfied until "justice rolls down like waters, and righteousness like a mighty stream."[1]

I am not unmindful that some of you have come here out of great trials and tribulations. Some of you have come fresh from narrow jail cells. And some of you have come from areas where your quest — quest for freedom left you battered by the storms of persecution and staggered by the winds of police brutality. You have been the veterans of creative suffering. Continue to work with the faith that unearned suffering is redemptive. Go back to Mississippi, go back to Alabama, go back to South Carolina, go back to Georgia, go back to Louisiana, go back to the slums and ghettos of our northern cities, knowing that somehow this situation can and will be changed.

Let us not wallow in the valley of despair, I say to you today, my friends.

And so even though we face the difficulties of today and tomorrow, I still have a dream. It is a dream deeply rooted in the American dream.

I have a dream that one day this nation will rise up and live out the true meaning of its creed: "We hold these truths to be self-evident, that all men are created equal."

I have a dream that one day on the red hills of Georgia, the sons of former slaves and the sons of former slave owners will be able to sit down together at the table of brotherhood.

I have a dream that one day even the state of Mississippi, a state sweltering with the heat of injustice, sweltering with the heat of oppression, will be transformed into an oasis of freedom and justice.

I have a dream that my four little children will one day live in a nation where they will not be judged by the color of their skin but by the content of their character.

I have a dream today!

I have a dream that one day, down in Alabama, with its vicious racists, with its governor having his lips dripping with the words of "interposition" and "nullification" — one day right there in Alabama little black boys and black girls will be able to join hands with little white boys and white girls as sisters and brothers.

I have a dream today!

I have a dream that one day every valley shall be exalted, and every hill and mountain shall be made low, the rough places will be made plain, and the crooked places will be made straight; "and the glory of the Lord shall be revealed and all flesh shall see it together."[2]

This is our hope, and this is the faith that I go back to the South with.

With this faith, we will be able to hew out of the mountain of despair a stone of hope. With this faith, we will be able to transform the jangling discords of our nation into a beautiful symphony of brotherhood. With this faith, we will be able to work together, to pray together, to struggle together, to go to jail together, to stand up for freedom together, knowing that we will be free one day.

And this will be the day – this will be the day when all of God's children will be able to sing with new meaning:

My country 'tis of thee, sweet land of liberty, of thee I sing.

Land where my fathers died, land of the Pilgrim's pride,

From every mountainside, let freedom ring!

And if America is to be a great nation, this must become true.

And so let freedom ring from the prodigious hilltops of New Hampshire.

Let freedom ring from the mighty mountains of New York.

Let freedom ring from the heightening Alleghenies of Pennsylvania.

Let freedom ring from the snow-capped Rockies of Colorado.

Let freedom ring from the curvaceous slopes of California.

But not only that:

Let freedom ring from Stone Mountain of Georgia.

Let freedom ring from Lookout Mountain of Tennessee.

Let freedom ring from every hill and molehill of Mississippi.

From every mountainside, let freedom ring.

And when this happens, when we allow freedom ring, when we let it ring from every village and every hamlet, from every state and every city, we will be able to speed up that day when all of God's children, black men and white men, Jews and Gentiles, Protestants and Catholics, will be able to join hands and sing in the words of the old Negro spiritual:

Free at last! Free at last!

Thank God Almighty, we are free at last!

"Pearl Harbor Address to the Nation"
by Franklin D. Roosevelt

December 8, 1941

Mr. Vice President, Mr. Speaker, Members of the Senate, and of the House of Representatives:

Yesterday, December 7th, 1941 — a date which will live in infamy — the United States of America was suddenly and deliberately attacked by naval and air forces of the Empire of Japan.

The United States was at peace with that nation and, at the solicitation of Japan, was still in conversation with its government and its emperor looking toward the maintenance of peace in the Pacific.

Indeed, one hour after Japanese air squadrons had commenced bombing in the American island of Oahu, the Japanese ambassador to the United States and his colleague delivered to our Secretary of State a formal reply to a recent American message. And while this reply stated that it seemed useless to continue the existing diplomatic negotiations, it contained no threat or hint of war or of armed attack.

It will be recorded that the distance of Hawaii from Japan makes it obvious that the attack was deliberately planned many days or even weeks ago. During the intervening time, the Japanese government has deliberately sought to deceive the United States by false statements and expressions of hope for continued peace.

The attack yesterday on the Hawaiian Islands has caused severe damage to American naval and military forces. I regret to tell you that very many American lives have been lost. In addition, American ships have been reported torpedoed on the high seas between San Francisco and Honolulu.

Yesterday, the Japanese government also launched an attack against Malaya.

Last night, Japanese forces attacked Hong Kong.

Last night, Japanese forces attacked Guam.

Last night, Japanese forces attacked the Philippine Islands.

Last night, the Japanese attacked Wake Island.

And this morning, the Japanese attacked Midway Island.

Japan has, therefore, undertaken a surprise offensive extending throughout the Pacific area. The facts of yesterday and today speak for themselves. The people of the United States have already formed their opinions and well understand the implications to the very life and safety of our nation.

As commander in chief of the Army and Navy, I have directed that all measures be taken for our defense. But always will our whole nation remember the character of the onslaught against us.

No matter how long it may take us to overcome this premeditated invasion, the American people in their righteous might will win through to absolute victory.

I believe that I interpret the will of the Congress and of the people when I assert that we will not only defend ourselves to the uttermost, but will make it very certain that this form of treachery shall never again endanger us.

Hostilities exist. There is no blinking at the fact that our people, our territory, and our interests are in grave danger.

With confidence in our armed forces, with the unbounding determination of our people, we will gain the inevitable triumph — so help us God.

I ask that the Congress declare that since the unprovoked and dastardly attack by Japan on Sunday, December 7th, 1941, a state of war has existed between the United States and the Japanese empire.

"Blood, Toil, Sweat, and Tears"
by Winston Churchill

May 13, 1940

Mr. Speaker:

On Friday evening last I received His Majesty's commission to form a new Administration. It was the evident wish and will of Parliament and the nation that this should be conceived on the broadest possible basis and that it should include all parties, both those who supported the late Government and also the parties of the Opposition.

I have completed the most important part of this task. A War Cabinet has been formed of five Members, representing, with the Liberal Opposition, the unity of the nation. The three party Leaders have agreed to serve, either in the War Cabinet or in high executive office. The three Fighting Services have been filled. It was necessary that this should be done in one single day, on account of the extreme urgency and rigor of events. A number of other key positions were filled yesterday, and I am submitting a further list to His Majesty tonight. I hope to complete the appointment of the principal Ministers during tomorrow. The appointment of the other Ministers usually takes a little longer, but I trust that, when Parliament meets again, this part of my task will be completed, and that the Administration will be complete in all respects.

Sir, I considered it in the public interest to suggest that the House should be summoned to meet today. Mr. Speaker agreed and took the necessary steps, in accordance with the powers conferred upon him by the Resolution of the House. At the end of the proceedings today, the Adjournment of the House will be proposed until Tuesday, the 21st May, with, of course, provision for earlier meeting, if need be. The business to be considered during that week will be notified to Members at the earliest opportunity. I now invite the House, by the Resolution which stands in my name, to record its approval of the steps taken and to declare its confidence in the new Government.

Sir, to form an Administration of this scale and complexity is a serious undertaking in itself, but it must be remembered that we are in the preliminary stage of one of the greatest battles in history, that we are in action at many points in Norway and in Holland, that we have to be prepared in the Mediterranean, that the air battle is continuous and that many preparations have to be made here at home. In this crisis I hope I may be pardoned if I do not address the House at any length today. I hope that any of my friends and colleagues, or former colleagues, who are affected by the political reconstruction, will make all allowances for any lack of ceremony with which it has been necessary to act. I would say to the House, as I said to those who've joined this government: "I have nothing to offer but blood, toil, tears and sweat."

We have before us an ordeal of the most grievous kind. We have before us many, many long months of struggle and of suffering. You ask, what is our policy? I will say: It is to wage war, by sea, land and air, with all our might and with all the strength that God can give us; to wage war against a monstrous tyranny, never surpassed in the dark and lamentable catalogue of human crime. That is our policy. You ask, what is our aim? I can answer in one word: victory. Victory at all costs, victory in spite of all terror, victory, however long and hard the road may be; for without victory, there is no survival. Let that be realized; no survival for the British Empire, no survival for all that the British Empire has stood for, no survival for the urge and impulse of the ages, that mankind will move forward towards its goal.

But I take up my task with buoyancy and hope. I feel sure that our cause will not be suffered to fail among men. At this time I feel entitled to claim the aid of all, and I say, "Come then, let us go forward together with our united strength."

"The Right of the People to Rule"
by Theodore Roosevelt

March 20, 1912

Carnegie Hall, New York City

The great fundamental issue now before the Republican Party and before our people can be stated briefly. It is: Are the American people fit to govern themselves, to rule themselves, to control themselves? I believe they are. My opponents do not. I believe in the right of the people to rule. I believe the majority of the plain people of the United States will, day in and day out, make fewer mistakes in governing themselves than any smaller class or body of men, no matter what their training, will make in trying to govern them. I believe, again, that the American people are, as a whole, capable of self-control and of learning by their mistakes. Our opponents pay lip-loyalty to this doctrine; but they show their real beliefs by the way in which they champion every device to make the nominal rule of the people a sham. I have scant patience with this talk of the tyranny of the majority. Wherever there is tyranny of the majority, I shall protest against it with all my heart and soul. But we are today suffering from the tyranny of minorities. It is a small minority that is grabbing our coal-deposits, our water-powers, and our harbor fronts. A small minority is battening on the sale of adulterated foods and drugs. It is a small minority that lies behind monopolies and trusts. It is a small minority that stands behind the present law of master and servant, the sweat-shops, and the whole calendar of social and industrial injustice. It is a small minority that is today using our convention system to defeat the will of a majority of the people in the choice of delegates to the Chicago Convention.

The only tyrannies from which men, women, and children are suffering in real life are the tyrannies of minorities. If the majority of the American people were in fact tyrannous over the minority, if democracy had no greater self-control than empire, then indeed no written words which our forefathers put into the Constitution could stay that tyranny.

No sane man who has been familiar with the government of this country for the last twenty years will complain that we have had too much of the rule of the majority. The trouble has been a far different one that, at many times and in many localities, there have held public office in the States and in the nation men who have, in fact, served not the whole people, but some special class or special interest. I am not thinking only of those special interests which by grosser methods, by bribery and crime, have stolen from the people. I am thinking as much of their respectable allies and figureheads, who have ruled and legislated and decided as if in some way the vested rights of privilege had a first mortgage on the whole United States, while the rights of all the people were merely an unsecured debt. Am I overstating the case? Have our political leaders always, or generally, recognized their duty to the people as anything more than a duty to disperse the mob, see that the ashes are taken away, and distribute patronage? Have our leaders always, or generally, worked for the benefit of human beings, to increase the prosperity of all the people, to give each some opportunity of living decently and bringing up his children well? The questions need no answer.

Now there has sprung up a feeling deep in the hearts of the people not of the bosses and professional politicians, not of the beneficiaries of special privilege-a pervading belief of thinking men that when the majority of the people do in fact, as well as theory, rule, then the servants of the people will come more quickly to answer and obey, not the commands of the special interests, but those of the whole people. To reach toward that end the Progressives of the Republican Party in certain States have formulated certain proposals for change in the form of the State government – certain new "checks and balances" which may check and balance the special interests and their allies. That is their purpose. Now turn for a moment to their proposed methods.

First, there are the "initiative and referendum," which are so framed that if the legislatures obey the command of some special interest, and obstinately refuse the will of the majority, the majority may step in and legislate directly. No man would say that it was best to conduct all legislation by direct vote of the people-it would mean the loss of deliberation, of patient consideration but, on the other hand, no one whose mental arteries have not long since hardened can doubt that the proposed changes are needed when the legislatures refuse to carry out the will of the people. The proposal is a method to reach an undeniable evil. Then there is the recall of public officers the principle that an officer chosen by the people who is unfaithful may be recalled by vote of the majority before he finishes his term. I will speak of the recall of judges in a moment – leave that aside – but as to the other officers, I have heard no argument advanced against the proposition, save that it will make the public officer timid and always currying favor with the mob. That argument means that you can fool all the people all the time, and is an avowal of disbelief in democracy. If it is true and I believe it is not it is less important than to stop those public officers from currying favor with the interests. Certain States may need the recall, others may not; where the term of elective office is short it may be quite needless; but there are occasions when it meets a real evil, and provides a needed check and balance against the special interests.

Then there is the direct primary the real one, not the New

York one and that, too, the Progressives offer as a check on the special interests. Most clearly of all does it seem to me that this change is wholly good for every State. The system of party government is not written in our constitutions, but it is none the less a vital and essential part of our form of government. In that system the party leaders should serve and carry out the will of their own party. There is no need to show how far that theory is from the facts, or to rehearse the vulgar thieving partnerships of the corporations and the bosses, or to show how many times the real government lies in the hands of the boss, protected from the commands and the revenge of the voters by his puppets in office and the power of patronage. We need not be told how he is thus entrenched or how hard he is to overthrow. The facts stand out in the history of nearly every State in the Union. They are blots on our political system. The direct primary will give the voters a method ever ready to use, by which the party leader shall be made to obey their command. The direct primary, if accompanied by a stringent corrupt-practices act, will help break up the corrupt partnership of corporations and politicians.

My opponents charge that two things in my programme are wrong because they intrude into the sanctuary of the judiciary. The first is the recall of judges; and the second, the review by the people of, judicial decisions on certain constitutional questions. I have said again and again that I do not advocate the recall of judges in all States and in all communities. In my own State I do not advocate it or believe it to be needed, for in this State our trouble lies not with corruption on the bench, but with the effort by the honest but wrong-headed judges to thwart the people in their struggle for social justice and fair dealing. The integrity of our judges from Marshall to White and Holmes and to Cullen and many others in our own State is a fine page of American history. But I say it soberly democracy has a right to approach the sanctuary of the courts when a special interest has corruptly found sanctuary there; and this is exactly what has happened in some of the States where the recall of the judges is a living issue. I would far more willingly trust the whole people to judge such a case than some special tribunal-perhaps appointed by the same power that chose the judge if that tribunal is not itself really responsible to the people and is hampered and clogged by the technicalities of impeachment proceedings.

I have stated that the courts of the several States – not always but often – have construed the "due process" clause of the State constitutions as if it prohibited the whole people of the State from adopting methods of regulating the use of property so that human life, particularly the lives of the working men, shall be safer, freer, and happier. No one can successfully impeach this statement. I have insisted that the true construction of "due process" is that pronounced by Justice Holmes in delivering the unanimous opinion of the Supreme Court of the United States, when he said: "The police power extends to all the great public need. It may be put forth in aid of what is sanctioned by usage, or held by the prevailing morality or strong and preponderant opinion to be greatly and immediately necessary to the public welfare." I insist that the decision of the New York court of appeals in the Ives case, which set aside the will of the majority of the people as to the compensation of injured workmen in dangerous trades, was intolerable and based on a wrong political philosophy. I urge that in such cases where the courts construe the due process clause as if property rights, to the exclusion of human rights, had a first mortgage on the Constitution, the people may, after sober deliberation, vote, and finally determine whether the law which the court set aside shall be valid or not. By this method can be clearly and finally ascertained the preponderant opinion of the people which Justice Holmes makes the test of due process in the case of laws enacted in the exercise of the police power. The ordinary methods now in vogue of amending the Constitution have in actual practice proved wholly inadequate to secure justice in such cases with reasonable speed, and cause intolerable delay and injustice, and those who stand against the changes I propose are champions of wrong and injustice, and of tyranny by the wealthy and the strong over the weak and the helpless.

So that no man may misunderstand me, let me recapitulate:

I am not proposing anything in connection with the Supreme Court of the United States, or with the Federal Constitution.

I am not proposing anything having any connection with ordinary suits, civil or criminal, as between individuals.

I am not speaking of the recall of judges.

I am proposing merely that in a certain class of cases involving police power, when a State court has set aside as unconstitutional a law passed by the legislature for the general welfare, the question of the validity of the law, which should depend, as Justice Holmes so well phrases it, upon the prevailing morality or preponderant opinion be submitted for final determination to a vote of the people, taken after due time for consideration.

And I contend that the people, in the nature of things, must be better judges of what is the preponderant opinion than the courts, and that the courts should not be allowed to reverse the political philosophy of the people. My point is well illustrated by a recent decision of the Supreme Court, holding that the court would not take jurisdiction of a case involving the constitutionality of the initiative and referendum laws of Oregon. The ground of the decision was that such a question was not judicial in its nature, but should be left for determination to the other coordinate departments of the government. Is it not equally plain that the question whether a given social policy is for the public good is not of a judicial nature, but should be settled by the legislature or in the final instance by the people themselves?

The President of the United States, Mr. Taft, devoted most of a recent speech to criticism of this proposition. He says that it "is utterly without merit or utility, and, instead of being in the interest of all the people, and of the stability of popular government, is sowing the seeds of confusion and tyranny." (By this he, of course, means the tyranny of the majority, that is, the tyranny of the American people as a whole.) He also says that my proposal (which, as he rightly sees, is merely a proposal to give the people a real, instead of only a nominal, chance to construe and amend a State constitution with reasonable rapidity) would make such amendment and interpretation "depend on the feverish, uncertain, and unstable determination of successive votes on different laws by temporary and changing majorities"; and that "it lays the axe at the root of the tree of well-ordered freedom, and subjects the guaranties of life, liberty, and property without remedy to the fitful impulse of a temporary majority of an electorate."

This criticism is really less a criticism of my proposal than a criticism of all popular government. It is wholly unfounded, unless it is founded on the belief that the people are fundamentally untrustworthy. If the Supreme Court's definition of due process in relation to the police power is sound, then an act of the legislature to promote the collective interests of the community must be valid, if it embodies a policy held by the prevailing morality or a preponderant opinion to be necessary to the public welfare.

This is the question that I propose to submit to the people. How can the prevailing morality or a preponderant opinion be better and more exactly ascertained than by a vote of the people?

The people must know better than the court what their own morality and their own opinion is. I ask that you, here, you and the others like you, you the people, be given the chance to state your own views of justice and public morality, and not sit meekly by and have your views announced for you by well-meaning adherents of outworn philosophies, who exalt the pedantry of formulas above the vital needs of human life.

The object I have in view could probably be accomplished by an amendment of the State constitutions taking away from the courts the power to review the legislature's determination of a policy of social justice, by defining due process of law in accordance with the views expressed by Justice Holmes of the Supreme Court. But my proposal seems to me more democratic and, I may add, less radical. For under the method I suggest the people may sustain the court as against the legislature, whereas, if due process were defined in the Constitution, the decision of the legislature would be final.

Mr. Taft's position is the position that has been held from the beginning of our government, although not always so openly held, by a large number of reputable and honorable men who, down at bottom, distrust popular government, and, when they must accept it, accept it with reluctance, and hedge it around with every species of restriction and check and balance, so as to make the power of the people as limited and as ineffective as possible.

Mr. Taft fairly defines the issue when he says that our government is and should be a government of all the people by a representative part of the people. This is an excellent and moderate description of all oligarchy. It defines our government as a government of all the people by a few of the people.

Mr. Taft, in his able speech, has made what is probably the

best possible presentation of the case for those who feel in this manner. Essentially this view differs only in its expression from the view nakedly set forth by one of his supporters, Congressman Campbell. Congressman Campbell, in a public speech in New Hampshire, in opposing the proposition to give the people real and effective control over all their servants, including the judges, stated that this was equivalent to allowing an appeal from the umpire to the bleachers. Doubtless Congressman Campbell was not himself aware of the cynical truthfulness with which he was putting the real attitude of those for whom he spoke. But it unquestionably is their real attitude. Mr. Campbell's conception of the part the American people should play in self-government is that they should sit on the bleachers and pay the price of admission, but should have nothing to say as to the contest which is waged in the arena by the professional politicians. Apparently Mr. Campbell ignores the fact that the American people are not mere onlookers at a game, that they have a vital stake in the contest, and that democracy means nothing unless they are able and willing to show that they are their own masters.

I am not speaking jokingly, nor do I mean to be unkind; for I repeat that many honorable and well-meaning men of high character take this view, and have taken it from the time of the formation of the nation. Essentially this view is that the Constitution is a straight-jacket to be used for the control of an unruly patient the people. Now, I hold that this view is not only false but mischievous, that our constitutions are instruments designed to secure justice by securing the deliberate but effective expression of the popular will, that the checks and balances are valuable as far, and only so far, as they accomplish that deliberation, and that it is a warped and unworthy and improper construction of our form of government to see in it only a means of thwarting the popular will and of preventing justice.

Mr. Taft says that "every class" should have a "voice" in the government. That seems to me a very serious misconception of the American political situation. The real trouble with us is that some classes have had too much voice. One of the most important of all the lessons to be taught and to be learned is that a man should vote, not as a representative of a class, but merely as a good citizen, whose prime interests are the same as those of all other good citizens. The belief in different classes, each having a voice in the government, has given rise to much of our present difficulty; for whosoever believes in these separate classes, each with a voice, inevitably, even although unconsciously, tends to work, not for the good of the whole people, but for the protection of some special class-usually that to which he himself belongs. The same principle applies when Mr. Taft says that the judiciary ought not to be "representative" of the people in the sense that the legislature and the Executive are. This is perfectly true of the judge when he is performing merely the ordinary functions of a judge in suits between man and man. It is not true of the judge engaged in interpreting, for instance, the due process clause where the judge is ascertaining the preponderant opinion of the people (as Judge Holmes states it). When he exercises that function he has no right to let his political philosophy reverse and thwart the will of the majority. In that function the judge must represent the people or he fails in the test the Supreme Court has laid down. Take the Workmen's Compensation Act here in New York. The legislators gave us a law in the interest of humanity and decency and fair dealing. In so doing they represented the people, and represented them well. Several judges declared that law constitutional in our State, and several courts in other States declared similar laws constitutional, and the Supreme Court of the nation declared a similar law affecting men in interstate business constitutional; but the highest court in the State of New York, the court of appeals, declared that we, the people of New York, could not have such a law. I hold that in this case the legislators and the judges alike occupied representative positions; the difference was merely that the former represented us well and the latter represented us ill. Remember that the legislators promised that law, and were returned by the people partly in consequence of such promise. That judgment of the people should not have been set aside unless it was irrational. Yet in the Ives case the New York court of appeals praised the policy of the law and the end it sought to obtain; and then declared that the people lacked power to do justice!

Mr. Taft again and again, in quotations I have given and elsewhere through his speech, expresses his disbelief in the people when they vote at the polls. In one sentence he says that the proposition gives "powerful effect to the momentary impulse of a majority of an electorate and prepares the way for the possible exercise of the grossest tyranny." Elsewhere he speaks of the "feverish uncertainty" and "unstable determination" of laws by "temporary and changing majorities"; and again he says that the system I propose "would result in suspension or application of constitutional guaranties according to popular whim," which would destroy "all possible consistency" in constitutional interpretation. I should much like to know the exact distinction that is to be made between what Mr. Taft calls "the fitful impulse of a temporary majority" when applied to a question such as that I raise and any other question. Remember that under my proposal to review a rule of decision by popular vote, amending or construing, to that extent, the Constitution, would certainly take at least two years from the time of the election of the legislature which passed the act. Now, only four months elapse between the nomination and the election of a man as President, to fill for four years the most important office in the land. In one of Mr. Taft's speeches he speaks of "the voice of the people as coming next to the voice of God." Apparently, then, the decision of the people about the presidency, after four months deliberation, is to be treated as "next to the voice of God"; but if, after two years of sober thought, they decide that women and children shall be protected in industry, or men protected from excessive hours of labor under unhygienic conditions, or wage-workers compensated when they lose life or limb in the service of others, then their decision forthwith becomes a "whim" and "feverish" and "unstable" and an exercise of "the grossest tyranny" and the "laying of the axe to the root of the tree of freedom."

It seems absurd to speak of a conclusion reached by the people after two years deliberation, after thrashing the matter out before the legislature, after thrashing it out before the governor, after thrashing it out before the court and by the court, and then after full debate for four or six months, as "the fitful impulse of a temporary majority." If Mr. Taft's language correctly describes such action by the people, then he himself and all other Presidents have been elected by "the fitful impulse of a temporary majority"; then the constitution of each State, and the Constitution of the nation, have been adopted, and all amendments thereto have been adopted, by "the fitful impulse of a temporary majority." If he is right, it was "the fitful impulse of a temporary majority" which founded, and another fitful impulse which perpetuated this nation.

Mr. Taft's position is perfectly clear. It is that we have in this country a special class of persons wiser than the people, who are above the people, who cannot be reached by the people, but who govern them and ought to govern them; and who protect various classes of the people from the whole people. That is the old, old doctrine which has been acted upon for thousands of years abroad; and which here in America has been acted upon sometimes openly, sometimes secretly, for forty years by many men in public and in private life, and I am sorry to say by many judges; a doctrine which has in fact tended to create a bulwark for privilege, a bulwark unjustly protecting special interests against the rights of the people as a whole. This doctrine is to me a dreadful doctrine; for its effect is, and can only be, to make the courts the shield of privilege against popular rights. Naturally, every upholder and beneficiary of crooked privilege loudly applauds the doctrine. It is behind the shield of that doctrine that crooked clauses creep into laws, those men of wealth and power control legislation. The men of wealth who praise this doctrine, this theory, would do well to remember that to its adoption by the courts is due the distrust so many of our wage-workers now feel for the courts. I deny that that theory has worked so well that we should continue it. I most earnestly urge that the evils and abuses it has produced cry aloud for remedy; and the only remedy is in fact to restore the power to govern directly to the people, and to make the public servant directly responsible to the whole people-and to no part of them, to no "class" of them.

Mr. Taft is very much afraid of the tyranny of majorities. For twenty-five years here in New York State, in our efforts to get social and industrial justice, we have suffered from the tyranny of a small minority. We have been denied, now by one court, now by another, as in the Bakeshop Case, where the courts set aside the law limiting the hours of labor in bakeries -the "due process" clause again as in the Workmen's Compensation Act, as in the Tenement House Cigar Factory Case in all these and many other cases we have been denied by small minorities, by a few worthy men of wrong political philosophy on the bench, the right to protect our people in their lives, their liberty, and their pursuit of happiness. As for "consistency "why, the record of the courts, in such a case as the income tax, for instance, is so full of inconsistencies as to make the fear expressed of "inconsistency" on the part of the people seem childish…

"Duty, Honor, Country"
by General Douglas MacArthur

May 12, 1962

General Westmoreland, General Grove, distinguished guests, and gentlemen of the Corps!

As I was leaving the hotel this morning, a doorman asked me, "Where are you bound for, General?" And when I replied, "West Point," he remarked, "Beautiful place. Have you ever been there before?"

No human being could fail to be deeply moved by such a tribute as this [Thayer Award]. Coming from a profession I have served so long, and a people I have loved so well, it fills me with an emotion I cannot express. But this award is not intended primarily to honor a personality, but to symbolize a great moral code — the code of conduct and chivalry of those who guard this beloved land of culture and ancient descent. That is the animation of this medallion. For all eyes and for all time, it is an expression of the ethics of the American soldier. That I should be integrated in this way with so noble an ideal arouses a sense of pride and yet of humility which will be with me always

Duty, Honor, Country: Those three hallowed words reverently dictate what you ought to be, what you can be, what you will be. They are your rallying points: to build courage when courage seems to fail; to regain faith when there seems to be little cause for faith; to create hope when hope becomes forlorn.

Unhappily, I possess neither that eloquence of diction, that poetry of imagination, nor that brilliance of metaphor to tell you all that they mean.

The unbelievers will say they are but words, but a slogan, but a flamboyant phrase. Every pedant, every demagogue, every cynic, every hypocrite, every troublemaker, and I am sorry to say, some others of an entirely different character, will try to downgrade them even to the extent of mockery and ridicule.

But these are some of the things they do. They build your basic character. They mold you for your future roles as the custodians of the nation's defense. They make you strong enough to know when you are weak, and brave enough to face yourself when you are afraid. They teach you to be proud and unbending in honest failure, but humble and gentle in success; not to substitute words for actions, not to seek the path of comfort, but to face the stress and spur of difficulty and challenge; to learn to stand up in the storm but to have compassion on those who fall; to master yourself before you seek to master others; to have a heart that is clean, a goal that is high; to learn to laugh, yet never forget how to weep; to reach into the future yet never neglect the past; to be serious yet never to take yourself too seriously; to be modest so that you will remember the simplicity of true greatness, the open mind of true wisdom, the meekness of true strength. They give you a temper of the will, a quality of the imagination, a vigor of the emotions, a freshness of the deep springs of life, a temperamental predominance of courage over timidity, of an appetite for adventure over love of ease. They create in your heart the sense of wonder, the unfailing hope of what next, and the joy and inspiration of life. They teach you in this way to be an officer and a gentleman.

And what sort of soldiers are those you are to lead? Are they reliable? Are they brave? Are they capable of victory? Their story is known to all of you. It is the story of the American man-at-arms. My estimate of him was formed on the battlefield many, many years ago, and has never changed. I regarded him then as I regard him now — as one of the world's noblest figures, not only as one of the finest military characters, but also as one of the most stainless. His name and fame are the birthright of every American citizen. In his youth and strength, his love and loyalty, he gave all that mortality can give.

He needs no eulogy from me or from any other man. He has written his own history and written it in red on his enemy's breast. But when I think of his patience under adversity, of his courage under fire, and of his modesty in victory, I am filled with an emotion of admiration I cannot put into words. He belongs to history as furnishing one of the greatest examples of successful patriotism. He belongs to posterity as the instructor of future generations in the principles of liberty and freedom. He belongs to the present, to us, by his virtues and by his achievements. In 20 campaigns, on a hundred battlefields, around a thousand campfires, I have witnessed that enduring fortitude, that patriotic self-abnegation, and that invincible determination which have carved his statue in the hearts of his people. From one end of the world to the other he has drained deep the chalice of courage.

As I listened to those songs [of the glee club], in memory's eye I could see those staggering columns of the First World War, bending under soggy packs, on many a weary march from dripping dusk to drizzling dawn, slogging ankle-deep through the mire of shell-shocked roads, to form grimly for the attack, blue-lipped, covered with sludge and mud, chilled by the wind and rain, driving home to their objective, and for many, to the judgment seat of God.

I do not know the dignity of their birth, but I do know the glory of their death. They died unquestioning, uncomplaining, with faith in their hearts, and on their lips the hope that we would go on to victory. Always, for them: Duty, Honor, Country; always their blood and sweat and tears, as we sought the way and the light and the truth.

And 20 years after, on the other side of the globe, again the filth of murky foxholes, the stench of ghostly trenches, the slime of dripping dugouts; those boiling suns of relentless heat, those torrential rains of devastating storms; the loneliness and utter desolation of jungle trails; the bitterness of long separation from those they loved and cherished; the deadly pestilence of tropical disease; the horror of stricken areas of war; their resolute and determined defense, their swift and sure attack, their indomitable purpose, their complete and decisive victory — always victory. Always through the bloody haze of their last reverberating shot, the vision of gaunt, ghastly men reverently following your password of: Duty, Honor, Country.

The code which those words perpetuate embraces the highest moral laws and will stand the test of any ethics or philosophies ever promulgated for the uplift of mankind. Its requirements are for the things that are right, and its restraints are from the things that are wrong.

The soldier, above all other men, is required to practice the greatest act of religious training — sacrifice.

In battle and in the face of danger and death, he discloses those divine attributes which his Maker gave when he created man in his own image. No physical courage and no brute instinct can take the place of the Divine help which alone can sustain him.

However horrible the incidents of war may be, the soldier who is called upon to offer and to give his life for his country is the noblest development of mankind.

You now face a new world — a world of change. The thrust into outer space of the satellite, spheres, and missiles mark the beginning of another epoch in the long story of mankind. In the five or more billions of years the scientists tell us it has taken to form the earth, in the three or more billion years of development of the human race, there has never been a more abrupt or staggering evolution. We deal now not with things of this world alone, but with the illimitable distances and as yet unfathomed mysteries of the universe. We are reaching out for a new and boundless frontier.

We speak in strange terms: of harnessing the cosmic energy; of making winds and tides work for us; of creating unheard synthetic materials to supplement or even replace our old standard basics; to purify sea water for our drink; of mining ocean floors for new fields of wealth and food; of disease preventatives to expand life into the hundreds of years; of controlling the weather for a more equitable distribution of heat and cold, of rain and shine; of space ships to the moon; of the primary target in war, no longer limited to the armed forces of an enemy, but instead to include his civil populations; of ultimate conflict between a united human race and the sinister forces of some other planetary galaxy; of such dreams and fantasies as to make life the most exciting of all time.

And through all this welter of change and development, your mission remains fixed, determined, inviolable: it is to win our wars.

Everything else in your professional career is but corollary to this vital dedication. All other public purposes, all other public projects, all other public needs, great or small, will find others for their accomplishment. But you are the ones who are trained to fight. Yours is the profession of arms, the will to win, the sure knowledge that in war there is no substitute for victory; that if you lose, the nation will be destroyed; that the very obsession of your public service must be: Duty, Honor, Country.

Others will debate the controversial issues, national and international, which divide men's minds; but serene, calm, aloof, you stand as the Nation's war-guardian, as its lifeguard from the raging tides of international conflict, as its gladiator in the arena of battle. For a century and a half you have defended, guarded, and protected its hallowed traditions of liberty and freedom, of right and justice.

Let civilian voices argue the merits or demerits of our processes of government; whether our strength is being sapped by deficit financing, indulged in too long, by federal paternalism grown too mighty, by power groups grown too arrogant, by politics grown too corrupt, by crime grown too rampant, by morals grown too low, by taxes grown too high, by extremists grown too violent; whether our personal liberties are as thorough and complete as they should be. These great national problems are not for your professional participation or military solution. Your guidepost stands out like a ten-fold beacon in the night: Duty, Honor, Country.

You are the leaven which binds together the entire fabric of our national system of defense. From your ranks come the great captains who hold the nation's destiny in their hands the moment the war tocsin sounds. The Long Gray Line has never failed us. Were you to do so, a million ghosts in olive drab, in brown khaki, in blue and gray, would rise from their white crosses thundering those magic words: Duty, Honor, Country.

This does not mean that you are war mongers.

On the contrary, the soldier, above all other people, prays for peace, for he must suffer and bear the deepest wounds and scars of war.

But always in our ears ring the ominous words of Plato, that wisest of all philosophers: "Only the dead have seen the end of war."

The shadows are lengthening for me. The twilight is here. My days of old have vanished, tone and tint. They have gone glimmering through the dreams of things that were. Their memory is one of wondrous beauty, watered by tears, and coaxed and caressed by the smiles of yesterday. I listen vainly, but with thirsty ears, for the witching melody of faint bugles blowing reveille, of far drums beating the long roll. In my dreams I hear again the crash of guns, the rattle of musketry, the strange, mournful mutter of the battlefield.

But in the evening of my memory, always I come back to West Point.

Always there echoes and re-echoes: Duty, Honor, Country.

Today marks my final roll call with you, but I want you to know that when I cross the river my last conscious thoughts will be of The Corps, and The Corps, and The Corps.

I bid you farewell.

"The Decision to Go to the Moon" by John F. Kennedy

May 25, 1961

President Pitzer, Mr. Vice President, Governor, Congressman Thomas, Senator Wiley, and Congressman Miller, Mr. Webb, Mr. Bell, scientists, distinguished guests, and ladies and gentlemen:

I appreciate your president having made me an honorary visiting professor, and I will assure you that my first lecture will be very brief.

I am delighted to be here and I'm particularly delighted to be here on this occasion.

We meet at a college noted for knowledge, in a city noted for progress, in a state noted for strength, and we stand in need of all three, for we meet in an hour of change and challenge, in a decade of hope and fear, in an age of both knowledge and ignorance. The greater our knowledge increases, the greater our ignorance unfolds.

Despite the striking fact that most of the scientists that the world has ever known are alive and working today, despite the fact that this Nation's own scientific manpower is doubling every 12 years in a rate of growth more than three times that of our population as a whole, despite that, the vast stretches of the unknown and the unanswered and the unfinished still far outstrip our collective comprehension.

No man can fully grasp how far and how fast we have come, but condense, if you will, the 50,000 years of man's recorded history in a time span of but a half-century. Stated in these terms, we know very little about the first 40 years, except at the end of them advanced man had learned to use the skins of animals to cover them. Then about 10 years ago, under this standard, man emerged from his caves to construct other kinds of shelter. Only five years ago man learned to write and use a cart with wheels. Christianity began less than two years ago. The printing press came this year, and then less than two months ago, during this whole 50-year span of human history, the steam engine provided a new source of power. Newton explored the meaning of gravity. Last month electric lights and telephones and automobiles and airplanes became available. Only last week did we develop penicillin and television and nuclear power, and now if America's new spacecraft succeeds in reaching Venus, we will have literally reached the stars before midnight tonight.

This is a breathtaking pace, and such a pace cannot help but create new ills as it dispels old, new ignorance, new problems, new dangers. Surely the opening vistas of space promise high costs and hardships, as well as high reward.

So it is not surprising that some would have us stay where we are a little longer to rest, to wait. But this city of Houston, this state of Texas, this country of the United States was not built by those who waited and rested and wished to look behind them. This country was conquered by those who moved forward–and so will space.

William Bradford, speaking in 1630 of the founding of the Plymouth Bay Colony, said that all great and honorable actions are accompanied with great difficulties, and both must be enterprise and overcome with answerable courage.

If this capsule history of our progress teaches us anything, it is that man, in his quest for knowledge and progress, is determined and cannot be deterred. The exploration of space will go ahead, whether we join in it or not, and it is one of the great adventures of all time, and no nation which expects to be the leader of other nations can expect to stay behind in this race for space.

Those who came before us made certain that this country rode the first waves of the industrial revolution, the first waves of modern invention, and the first wave of nuclear power, and this generation does not intend to founder in the backwash of the coming age of space. We mean to be a part of it—we mean to lead it. For the eyes of the world now look into space, to the moon and to the planets beyond, and we have vowed that we shall not see it governed by a hostile flag of conquest, but by a banner of freedom and peace. We have vowed that we shall not see space filled with weapons of mass destruction, but with instruments of knowledge and understanding.

Yet the vows of this Nation can only be fulfilled if we in this Nation are first, and, therefore, we intend to be first. In short, our leadership in science and industry, our hopes for peace and security, our obligations to ourselves as well as others, all requires us to make this effort, to solve these mysteries, to solve them for the good of all men, and to become the world's leading space-faring nation.

We set sail on this new sea because there is new knowledge to be gained, and new rights to be won, and they must be won and used for the progress of all people. For space science, like nuclear science and all technology, has no conscience of its own. Whether it will become a force for good or ill depends on man, and only if the United States occupies a position of pre-eminence can we help decide whether this new ocean will be a sea of peace or a new terrifying theater of war. I do not say that we should or will go unprotected against the hostile misuse of space any more than we go unprotected against the hostile use of land or sea, but I do say that space can be explored and mastered without feeding the fires of war, without repeating the mistakes that man has made in extending his writ around this globe of ours.

There is no strife, no prejudice, no national conflict in outer space as yet. Its hazards are hostile to us all. Its conquest deserves the best of all mankind, and its opportunity for peaceful cooperation many never come again. But why, some say, the moon? Why choose this as our goal? And they may well ask why climb the highest mountain? Why, 35 years ago, fly the Atlantic? Why does Rice play Texas?

We choose to go to the moon. We choose to go to the moon in this decade and do the other things, not because they are easy, but because they are hard, because that goal will serve to organize and measure the best of our energies and skills, because that challenge is one that we are willing to accept, one we are unwilling to postpone, and one which we intend to win, and the others, too.

It is for these reasons that I regard the decision last year to shift our efforts in space from low to high gear as among the most important decisions that will be made during my incumbency in the office of the Presidency.

In the last 24 hours we have seen facilities now being created for the greatest and most complex exploration in man's history. We have felt the ground shake and the air shattered by the testing of a Saturn C-1 booster rocket, many times as powerful as the Atlas which launched John Glenn, generating power equivalent to 10,000 automobiles with their accelerators on the floor. We have seen the site where five F-1 rocket engines, each one as powerful as all eight engines of the Saturn combined, will be clustered together to make the advanced Saturn missile, assembled in a new building to be built at Cape Canaveral as tall as a 48 story structure, as wide as a city block, and as long as two lengths of this field.

Within these last 19 months at least 45 satellites have circled the earth. Some 40 of them were made in the United States of

America and they were far more sophisticated and supplied far more knowledge to the people of the world than those of the Soviet Union.

The Mariner spacecraft now on its way to Venus is the most intricate instrument in the history of space science. The accuracy of that shot is comparable to firing a missile from Cape Canaveral and dropping it in this stadium between the 40-yard lines.

Transit satellites are helping our ships at sea to steer a safer course. Trio's satellites have given us unprecedented warnings of hurricanes and storms, and will do the same for forest fires and icebergs.

We have had our failures, but so have others, even if they do not admit them. And they may be less public.

To be sure, we are behind, and will be behind for some time in manned flight. But we do not intend to stay behind, and in this decade, we shall make up and move ahead.

The growth of our science and education will be enriched by new knowledge of our universe and environment, by new techniques of learning and mapping and observation, by new tools and computers for industry, medicine, the home as well as the school. Technical institutions, such as Rice, will reap the harvest of these gains.

And finally, the space effort itself, while still in its infancy, has already created a great number of new companies, and tens of thousands of new jobs. Space and related industries are generating new demands in investment and skilled personnel, and this city and this state, and this region, will share greatly in this growth. What was once the furthest outpost on the old frontier of the West will be the furthest outpost on the new frontier of science and space. Houston, your city of Houston, with its Manned Spacecraft Center, will become the heart of a large scientific and engineering community. During the next 5 years the National Aeronautics and Space Administration expects to double the number of scientists and engineers in this area, to increase its outlays for salaries and expenses to $60 million a year; to invest some $200 million in plant and laboratory facilities; and to direct or contract for new space efforts over $1 billion from this center in this city.

To be sure, all this costs us all a good deal of money. This year's space budget is three times what it was in January 1961, and it is greater than the space budget of the previous eight years combined. That budget now stands at $540 million a year—a staggering sum, though somewhat less than we pay for cigarettes and cigars every year. Space expenditures will soon rise some more, from 40 cents per person per week to more than 50 cents a week for every man, woman and child in the United States, for we have given this program a high national priority—even though I realize that this is in some measure an act of faith and vision, for we do not now know what benefits await us. But if I were to say, my fellow citizens, that we shall send to the moon, 240,000 miles away from the control station in Houston, a giant rocket more than 300 feet tall, the length of this football field, made of new metal alloys, some of which have not yet been invented, capable of standing heat and stresses several times more than have ever been experienced, fitted together with a precision better than the finest watch, carrying all the equipment needed for propulsion, guidance, control, communications, food and survival, on an untried mission, to an unknown celestial body, and then return it safely to earth, re-entering the atmosphere at speeds of over 25,000 miles per hour, causing heat about half that of the temperature of the sun—almost as hot as it is here today—and do all this, and do it right, and do it first before this decade is out—then we must be bold.

I'm the one who is doing all the work, so we just want you to stay cool for a minute.

However, I think we're going to do it, and I think that we must pay what needs to be paid. I don't think we ought to waste any money, but I think we ought to do the job. And this will be done in the decade of the Sixties. It may be done while some of you are still here at school at this college and university. It will be done during the terms of office of some of the people who sit here on this platform. But it will be done. And it will be done before the end of this decade.

And I am delighted that this university is playing a part in putting a man on the moon as part of a great national effort of the United States of America.

Many years ago the great British explorer George Mallory, who was to die on Mount Everest, was asked why did he want to climb it. He said, "Because it is there."

Well, space is there, and we're going to climb it, and the moon and the planets are there, and new hopes for knowledge and peace are there. And, therefore, as we set sail we ask God's blessing on the most hazardous and dangerous and greatest adventure on which man has ever embarked.

Thank you.

"Give Me Liberty or Give Me Death"
by Patrick Henry

March 23, 1775

No man thinks more highly than I do of the patriotism, as well as abilities, of the very worthy gentlemen who have just addressed the House. But different men often see the same subject in different lights; and, therefore, I hope it will not be thought disrespectful to those gentlemen if, entertaining as I do opinions of a character very opposite to theirs, I shall speak forth my sentiments freely and without reserve. This is no time for ceremony. The questing before the House is one of awful moment to this country. For my own part, I consider it as nothing less than a question of freedom or slavery; and in proportion to the magnitude of the subject ought to be the freedom of the debate. It is only in this way that we can hope to arrive at truth, and fulfill the great responsibility which we hold to God and our country. Should I keep back my opinions at such a time, through fear of giving offense, I should consider myself as guilty of treason towards my country, and of an act of disloyalty toward the Majesty of Heaven, which I revere above all earthly kings.

Mr. President, it is natural to man to indulge in the illusions of hope. We are apt to shut our eyes against a painful truth, and listen to the song of that siren till she transforms us into beasts. Is this the part of wise men, engaged in a great and arduous struggle for liberty? Are we disposed to be of the number of those who, having eyes, see not, and, having ears, hear not, the things which so nearly concern their temporal salvation? For my part, whatever anguish of spirit it may cost, I am willing to know the whole truth; to know the worst, and to provide for it.

I have but one lamp by which my feet are guided, and that is the lamp of experience. I know of no way of judging of the future but by the past. And judging by the past, I wish to know what there has been in the conduct of the British ministry for the last ten years to justify those hopes with which gentlemen have been pleased to solace themselves and the House. Is it that insidious smile with which our petition has been lately received? Trust it not, sir; it will prove a snare to your feet. Suffer not yourselves to be betrayed with a kiss. Ask yourselves how this gracious reception of our petition comports with those warlike preparations which cover our waters and darken our land. Are fleets and armies necessary to a work of love and reconciliation? Have we shown ourselves so unwilling to be reconciled that force must be called in to win back our love? Let us not deceive ourselves, sir. These are the implements of war and subjugation; the last arguments to which kings resort. I ask gentlemen, sir, what means this martial array, if its purpose be not to force us to submission? Can gentlemen assign any other possible motive for it? Has Great Britain any enemy, in this quarter of the world, to call for all this accumulation of navies and armies? No, sir, she has none. They are meant for us: they can be meant for no other. They are sent over to bind and rivet upon us those chains which the British ministry have been so long forging. And what have we to oppose to them? Shall we try argument? Sir, we have been trying that for the last ten years. Have we anything new to offer upon the subject? Nothing. We have held the subject up in every light of which it is capable; but it has been all in vain. Shall we resort to entreaty and humble supplication? What terms shall we find which have not been already exhausted? Let us not, I beseech you, sir, deceive ourselves. Sir, we have done everything that could be done to avert the storm which is now coming on. We have petitioned; we have remonstrated; we have supplicated; we have prostrated ourselves before the throne, and have implored its interposition to arrest the tyrannical hands of the ministry and Parliament. Our petitions have been slighted; our remonstrances have produced additional violence and insult; our supplications have been disregarded; and we have been spurned, with contempt, from the foot of the throne! In vain, after these things, may we indulge the fond hope of peace and reconciliation. There is no longer any room for hope. If we wish to be free– if we mean to preserve inviolate those inestimable privileges for which we have been so long contending–if we mean not basely to abandon the noble struggle in which we have been so long engaged, and which we have pledged ourselves never to abandon until the glorious object of our contest shall be obtained–we must fight! I repeat it, sir, we must fight! An appeal to arms and to the God of hosts is all that is left us!

They tell us, sir, that we are weak; unable to cope with so formidable an adversary. But when shall we be stronger? Will it be the next week, or the next year? Will it be when we are totally disarmed, and when a British guard shall be stationed in every house? Shall we gather strength by irresolution and inaction? Shall we acquire the means of effectual resistance by lying supinely on our backs and hugging the delusive phantom of hope, until our enemies shall have bound us hand and foot? Sir, we are not weak if we make a proper use of those means which the God of nature hath placed in our power. The millions of people, armed in the holy cause of liberty, and in such a country as that which we possess, are invincible by any force which our enemy can send against us. Besides, sir, we shall not fight our battles alone. There is a just God who presides over the destinies of nations, and who will raise up friends to fight our battles for us. The battle, sir, is not to the strong alone; it is to the vigilant, the active, the brave. Besides, sir, we have no election. If we were base enough to desire it, it is now too late to retire from the contest. There is no retreat but in submission and slavery! Our chains are forged! Their clanking may be heard on the plains of Boston! The war is inevitable–and let it come! I repeat it, sir, let it come.

It is in vain, sir, to extenuate the matter. Gentlemen may cry, Peace, Peace– but there is no peace. The war is actually begun! The next gale that sweeps from the north will bring to our ears the clash of resounding arms! Our brethren are already in the field! Why stand we here idle? What is it that gentlemen wish? What would they have? Is life so dear, or peace so sweet, as to be purchased at the price of chains and slavery? Forbid it, Almighty God! I know not what course

"Remarks at the Brandenburg Gate" by Ronald Reagan

June 12, 1987

Thank you. Thank you, very much.

Chancellor Kohl, Governing Mayor Diepgen, ladies and gentlemen: Twenty four years ago, President John F. Kennedy visited Berlin, and speaking to the people of this city and the world at the city hall. Well since then two other presidents have come, each in his turn to Berlin. And today, I, myself, make my second visit to your city.

We come to Berlin, we American Presidents, because it's our duty to speak in this place of freedom. But I must confess, we're drawn here by other things as well; by the feeling of history in this city — more than 500 years older than our own nation; by the beauty of the Grunewald and the Tiergarten; most of all, by your courage and determination. Perhaps the composer, Paul Linke, understood something about American Presidents. You see, like so many Presidents before me, I come here today because wherever I go, whatever I do: "Ich hab noch einen Koffer in Berlin" [I still have a suitcase in Berlin.]

Our gathering today is being broadcast throughout Western Europe and North America. I understand that it is being seen and heard as well in the East. To those listening throughout Eastern Europe, I extend my warmest greetings and the good will of the American people. To those listening in East Berlin, a special word: Although I cannot be with you, I address my remarks to you just as surely as to those standing here before me. For I join you, as I join your fellow countrymen in the West, in this firm, this unalterable belief: Es gibt nur ein Berlin. [There is only one Berlin.]

Behind me stands a wall that encircles the free sectors of this city, part of a vast system of barriers that divides the entire continent of Europe. From the Baltic South, those barriers cut across Germany in a gash of barbed wire, concrete, dog runs, and guard towers. Farther south, there may be no visible, no obvious wall. But there remain armed guards and checkpoints all the same — still a restriction on the right to travel, still an instrument to impose upon ordinary men and women the will of a totalitarian state.

Yet, it is here in Berlin where the wall emerges most clearly; here, cutting across your city, where the news photo and the television screen have imprinted this brutal division of a continent upon the mind of the world.

Standing before the Brandenburg Gate, every man is a German separated from his fellow men.

Every man is a Berliner, forced to look upon a scar.

President Von WeizsÄocker has said, "The German question is open as long as the Brandenburg Gate is closed." Well today — today I say: As long as this gate is closed, as long as this scar of a wall is permitted to stand, it is not the German question alone that remains open, but the question of freedom for all mankind.

Yet, I do not come here to lament. For I find in Berlin a message of hope, even in the shadow of this wall, a message of triumph.

In this season of spring in 1945, the people of Berlin emerged from their air-raid shelters to find devastation. Thousands of miles away, the people of the United States reached out to help. And in 1947 Secretary of State — as you've been told — George Marshall announced the creation of what would become known as the Marshall Plan. Speaking precisely 40 years ago this month, he said: "Our policy is directed not against any country or doctrine, but against hunger, poverty, desperation, and chaos."

In the Reichstag a few moments ago, I saw a display commemorating this 40th anniversary of the Marshall Plan. I was struck by a sign — the sign on a burnt-out, gutted structure that was being rebuilt. I understand that Berliners of my own generation can remember seeing signs like it dotted throughout the western sectors of the city. The sign read simply: "The Marshall Plan is helping here to strengthen the free world." A strong, free world in the West — that dream became real. Japan rose from ruin to become an economic giant. Italy, France, Belgium — virtually every nation in Western Europe saw political and economic rebirth; the European Community was founded.

In West Germany and here in Berlin, there took place an economic miracle, the Wirtschaftswunder. Adenauer, Erhard, Reuter, and other leaders understood the practical importance of liberty — that just as truth can flourish only when the journalist is given freedom of speech, so prosperity can come about only when the farmer and businessman enjoy economic freedom. The German leaders — the German leaders reduced tariffs, expanded free trade, lowered taxes. From 1950 to 1960 alone, the standard of living in West Germany and Berlin doubled.

Where four decades ago there was rubble, today in West Berlin there is the greatest industrial output of any city in Germany: busy office blocks, fine homes and apartments, proud avenues, and the spreading lawns of parkland. Where a city's culture seemed to have been destroyed, today there are two great universities, orchestras and an opera, countless theaters, and museums. Where there was want, today there's abundance — food, clothing, automobiles — the wonderful goods of the Kudamm. From devastation, from utter ruin, you Berliners have, in freedom, rebuilt a city that once again ranks as one of the greatest on earth. Now the Soviets may have had other plans. But my friends, there were

THIRTEEN MOST PATRIOTIC SPEECHES IN AMERICAN HISTORY   145

a few things the Soviets didn't count on: Berliner Herz, Berliner Humor, ja, und Berliner Schnauze.

In the 1950s — In the 1950s Khrushchev predicted: "We will bury you."

But in the West today, we see a free world that has achieved a level of prosperity and well-being unprecedented in all human history. In the Communist world, we see failure, technological backwardness, declining standards of health, even want of the most basic kind — too little food. Even today, the Soviet Union still cannot feed itself. After these four decades, then, there stands before the entire world one great and inescapable conclusion: Freedom leads to prosperity. Freedom replaces the ancient hatreds among the nations with comity and peace. Freedom is the victor.

And now — now the Soviets themselves may, in a limited way, be coming to understand the importance of freedom. We hear much from Moscow about a new policy of reform and openness. Some political prisoners have been released. Certain foreign news broadcasts are no longer being jammed. Some economic enterprises have been permitted to operate with greater freedom from state control.

Are these the beginnings of profound changes in the Soviet state? Or are they token gestures intended to raise false hopes in the West, or to strengthen the Soviet system without changing it? We welcome change and openness; for we believe that freedom and security go together, that the advance of human liberty — the advance of human liberty can only strengthen the cause of world peace.

There is one sign the Soviets can make that would be unmistakable, that would advance dramatically the cause of freedom and peace.

General Secretary Gorbachev, if you seek peace, if you seek prosperity for the Soviet Union and Eastern Europe, if you seek liberalization: Come here to this gate.

Mr. Gorbachev, open this gate.

Mr. Gorbachev — Mr. Gorbachev, tear down this wall!

I understand the fear of war and the pain of division that afflict this continent, and I pledge to you my country's efforts to help overcome these burdens. To be sure, we in the West must resist Soviet expansion. So, we must maintain defenses of unassailable strength. Yet we seek peace; so we must strive to reduce arms on both sides.

Beginning 10 years ago, the Soviets challenged the Western alliance with a grave new threat, hundreds of new and more deadly SS-20 nuclear missiles capable of striking every capital in Europe. The Western alliance responded by committing itself to a counter-deployment (unless the Soviets agreed to negotiate a better solution) — namely, the elimination of such weapons on both sides. For many months, the Soviets refused to bargain in earnestness. As the alliance, in turn, prepared to go forward with its counter-deployment, there were difficult days, days of protests like those during my 1982 visit to this city; and the Soviets later walked away from the table.

But through it all, the alliance held firm. And I invite those who protested then — I invite those who protest today — to mark this fact: Because we remained strong, the Soviets came back to the table. Because we remained strong, today we have within reach the possibility, not merely of limiting the growth of arms, but of eliminating, for the first time, an entire class of nuclear weapons from the face of the earth.

As I speak, NATO ministers are meeting in Iceland to review the progress of our proposals for eliminating these weapons. At the talks in Geneva, we have also proposed deep cuts in strategic offensive weapons. And the Western allies have likewise made far-reaching proposals to reduce the danger of conventional war and to place a total ban on chemical weapons.

While we pursue these arms reductions, I pledge to you that we will maintain the capacity to deter Soviet aggression at any level at which it might occur. And in cooperation with many of our allies, the United States is pursuing the Strategic Defense Initiative — research to base deterrence not on the threat of offensive retaliation, but on defenses that truly defend; on systems, in short, that will not target populations, but shield them. By these means we seek to increase the safety of Europe and all the world. But we must remember a crucial fact: East and West do not mistrust each other because we are armed; we are armed because we mistrust each other. And our differences are not about weapons but about liberty. When President Kennedy spoke at the City Hall those 24 years ago, freedom was encircled; Berlin was under siege. And today, despite all the pressures upon this city, Berlin stands secure in its liberty. And freedom itself is transforming the globe.

In the Philippines, in South and Central America, democracy has been given a rebirth. Throughout the Pacific, free markets are working miracle after miracle of economic growth. In the industrialized nations, a technological revolution is taking place, a revolution marked by rapid, dramatic advances in computers and telecommunications.

In Europe, only one nation and those it controls refuse to join the community of freedom. Yet in this age of redoubled economic growth, of information and innovation, the Soviet Union faces a choice: It must make fundamental changes, or it will become obsolete.

148   LEFT - CENTER - RIGHT, WHAT IS BEST FOR AMERICA?

Today, thus, represents a moment of hope. We in the West stand ready to cooperate with the East to promote true openness, to break down barriers that separate people, to create a safer, freer world. And surely there is no better place than Berlin, the meeting place of East and West, to make a start.

Free people of Berlin: Today, as in the past, the United States stands for the strict observance and full implementation of all parts of the Four Power Agreement of 1971. Let us use this occasion, the 750th anniversary of this city, to usher in a new era, to seek a still fuller, richer life for the Berlin of the future. Together, let us maintain and develop the ties between the Federal Republic and the Western sectors of Berlin, which is permitted by the 1971 agreement.

And I invite Mr. Gorbachev: Let us work to bring the Eastern and Western parts of the city closer together, so that all the inhabitants of all Berlin can enjoy the benefits that come with life in one of the great cities of the world.

To open Berlin still further to all Europe, East and West, let us expand the vital air access to this city, finding ways of making commercial air service to Berlin more convenient, more comfortable, and more economical. We look to the day when West Berlin can become one of the chief aviation hubs in all central Europe.

With — With our French — With our French and British partners, the United States is prepared to help bring international meetings to Berlin. It would be only fitting for Berlin to serve as the site of United Nations meetings, or world conferences on human rights and arms control, or other issues that call for international cooperation.

There is no better way to establish hope for the future than to enlighten young minds, and we would be honored to sponsor summer youth exchanges, cultural events, and other programs for young Berliners from the East. Our French and British friends, I'm certain, will do the same. And it's my hope that an authority can be found in East Berlin to sponsor visits from young people of the Western sectors.

One final proposal, one close to my heart: Sport represents a source of enjoyment and ennoblement, and you may have noted that the Republic of Korea — South Korea — has offered to permit certain events of the 1988 Olympics to take place in the North. International sports competitions of all kinds could take place in both parts of this city. And what better way to demonstrate to the world the openness of this city than to offer in some future year to hold the Olympic Games here in Berlin, East and West.

In these four decades, as I have said, you Berliners have built a great city. You've done so in spite of threats — the Soviet attempts to impose the East-mark, the blockade. Today the city thrives in spite of the challenges implicit in the very presence of this wall. What keeps you here? Certainly there's a great deal to be said for your fortitude, for your defiant courage. But I believe there's something deeper, something that involves Berlin's whole look and feel and way of life — not mere sentiment. No one could live long in Berlin without being completely disabused of illusions. Something, instead, that has seen the difficulties of life in Berlin but chose to accept them, that continues to build this good and proud city in contrast to a surrounding totalitarian presence, that refuses to release human energies or aspirations, something that speaks with a powerful voice of affirmation, that says "yes" to this city, yes to the future, yes to freedom. In a word, I would submit that what keeps you in Berlin — is "love."

Love both profound and abiding.

Perhaps this gets to the root of the matter, to the most fundamental distinction of all between East and West. The totalitarian world produces backwardness because it does such violence to the spirit, thwarting the human impulse to create, to enjoy, to worship. The totalitarian world finds even symbols of love and of worship an affront.

Years ago, before the East Germans began rebuilding their churches, they erected a secular structure: the television tower at Alexander Platz. Virtually ever since, the authorities have been working to correct what they view as the tower's one major flaw: treating the glass sphere at the top with paints and chemicals of every kind. Yet even today when the sun strikes that sphere, that sphere that towers over all Berlin, the light makes the sign of the cross. There in Berlin, like the city itself, symbols of love, symbols of worship, cannot be suppressed.

As I looked out a moment ago from the Reichstag, that embodiment of German unity, I noticed words crudely spray-painted upon the wall, perhaps by a young Berliner (quote):

"This wall will fall. Beliefs become reality."

Yes, across Europe, this wall will fall, for it cannot withstand faith; it cannot withstand truth. The wall cannot withstand freedom.

And I would like, before I close, to say one word. I have read, and I have been questioned since I've been here about certain demonstrations against my coming. And I would like to say just one thing, and to those who demonstrate so. I wonder if they have ever asked themselves that if they should have the kind of government they apparently seek, no one would ever be able to do what they're doing again.

Thank you and God bless you all. Thank you.

Farewell Address of George Washington

December 23, 1783

Friends and Fellow Citizens:

The period for a new election of a citizen, to administer the executive government of the United States, being not far distant, and the time actually arrived, when your thoughts must be employed designating the person, who is to be clothed with that important trust, it appears to me proper, especially as it may conduce to a more distinct expression of the public voice, that I should now apprize you of the resolution I have formed, to decline being considered among the number of those out of whom a choice is to be made.

I beg you at the same time to do me the justice to be assured that this resolution has not been taken without a strict regard to all the considerations appertaining to the relation which binds a dutiful citizen to his country; and that in withdrawing the tender of service, which silence in my situation might imply, I am influenced by no diminution of zeal for your future interest, no deficiency of grateful respect for your past kindness, but am supported by a full conviction that the step is compatible with both.

The acceptance of, and continuance hitherto in, the office to which your suffrages have twice called me, have been a uniform sacrifice of inclination to the opinion of duty, and to a deference for what appeared to be your desire. I constantly hoped that it would have been much earlier in my power, consistently with motives, which I was not at liberty to disregard, to return to that retirement, from which I had been reluctantly drawn. The strength of my inclination to do this, previous to the last election, had even led to the preparation of an address to declare it to you; but mature reflection on the then perplexed and critical posture of our affairs with foreign nations, and the unanimous advice of persons entitled to my confidence impelled me to abandon the idea.

I rejoice, that the state of your concerns, external as well as internal, no longer renders the pursuit of inclination incompatible with the sentiment of duty, or propriety; and am persuaded, whatever partiality may be retained for my services, that, in the present circumstances of our country, you will not disapprove my determination to retire.

The impressions, with which I first undertook the arduous trust, were explained on the proper occasion. In the discharge of this trust, I will only say, that I have, with good intentions, contributed towards the organization and administration of the government the best exertions of which a very fallible judgment was capable. Not unconscious, in the outset, of the inferiority of my qualifications, experience in my own eyes, perhaps still more in the eyes of others, has strengthened the motives to diffidence of myself; and every day the increasing weight of years admonishes me more and more, that the shade of retirement is as necessary to me as it will be welcome. Satisfied, that, if any circumstances have given peculiar value to my services, they were temporary, I have the consolation to believe, that, while choice and prudence invite me to quit the political scene, patriotism does not forbid it.

In looking forward to the moment, which is intended to terminate the career of my public life, my feelings do not permit me to suspend the deep acknowledgment of that debt of gratitude, which I owe to my beloved country for the many honors it has conferred upon me; still more for the steadfast confidence with which it has supported me; and for the opportunities I have thence enjoyed of manifesting my inviolable attachment, by services faithful and persevering, though in usefulness unequal to my zeal. If benefits have resulted to our country from these services, let it always be remembered to your praise, and as an instructive example in our annals, that under circumstances in which the passions, agitated in every direction, were liable to mislead, amidst appearances sometimes dubious, vicissitudes of fortune often discouraging, in situations in which not infrequently want of success has countenanced the spirit of criticism, the constancy of your support was the essential prop of the efforts, and a guarantee of the plans by which they were effected. Profoundly penetrated with this idea, I shall carry it with me to my grave, as a strong incitement to unceasing vows that Heaven may continue to you the choicest tokens of its beneficence; that your union and brotherly affection may be perpetual; that the free constitution, which is the work of your hands, may be sacredly maintained; that its administration in every department may be stamped with wisdom and virtue; then, in fine, the happiness of the people of these States, under the auspices of liberty, may be made complete, by so careful a preservation and so prudent a use of this blessing, as will acquire to them the glory of recommending it to the applause, the affection, and adoption of every nation, which is yet a stranger to it.

Here, perhaps I ought to stop. But a solicitude for your welfare which cannot end but with my life, and the apprehension of danger, natural to that solicitude, urge me, on an occasion like the present, to offer to your solemn contemplation, and to recommend to your frequent review, some sentiments which are the result of much reflection, of no inconsiderable observation, and which appear to me all-important to the permanency of your felicity as a people. These will be offered to you with the more freedom, as you can only see in them the disinterested warnings of a parting friend, who can possibly have no personal motive to bias his counsel. Nor can I forget, as an encouragement to it, your indulgent reception of my sentiments on a former and not dissimilar occasion.

Interwoven as is the love of liberty with every ligament of your hearts, no recommendation of mine is necessary to fortify or confirm the attachment.

The unity of Government, which constitutes you one people, is also now dear to you. It is justly so; for it is a main pillar in the edifice of your real independence, the support of your tranquility at home, your peace abroad; of your safety; of your prosperity; of that very Liberty, which you so highly prize. But as it is easy to foresee, that, from different causes and from different quarters, much pains will be taken, many artifices employed, to weaken in your minds the conviction of this truth; as this is the point in your political fortress against which the batteries of internal and external enemies will be most constantly and actively (though often covertly and insidiously) directed, it is of infinite moment, that you should properly estimate the immense value of your national Union to your collective and individual happiness; that you should cherish a cordial, habitual, and immovable attachment to it; accustoming yourselves to think and speak of it as of the Palladium of your political safety and prosperity; watching for its preservation with jealous anxiety; discountenancing whatever may suggest even a suspicion, that it can in any event be abandoned; and indignantly frowning upon the first dawning of every attempt to alienate any portion of our country from the rest, or to enfeeble the sacred ties which now link together the various parts.

For this you have every inducement of sympathy and interest. Citizens, by birth or choice, of a common country, that country has a right to concentrate your affections. The name of American, which belongs to you, in your national capacity, must always exalt the just pride of Patriotism, more than any appellation derived from local discriminations. With slight shades of difference, you have the same religion, manners, habits, and political principles. You have in a common cause fought and triumphed together; the Independence and Liberty you possess are the work of joint counsels, and joint efforts, of common dangers, sufferings, and successes.

But these considerations, however powerfully they address themselves to your sensibility, are greatly outweighed by those, which apply more immediately to your interest. Here every portion of our country finds the most commanding motives for carefully guarding and preserving the Union of the whole.

The North, in an unrestrained intercourse with the South, protected by the equal laws of a common government, finds, in the productions of the latter, great additional resources of maritime and commercial enterprise and precious materials of manufacturing industry. The South, in the same intercourse, benefiting by the agency of the North, sees its agriculture grow and its commerce expand. Turning partly into its own channels the seamen of the North, it finds its particular navigation invigorated; and, while it contributes, in different ways, to nourish and increase the general mass of the national navigation, it looks forward to the protection of a maritime strength, to which itself is unequally adapted. The East, in a like intercourse with the West, already finds, and in the progressive improvement of interior communications by land and water, will more and more find, a valuable vent for the commodities which it brings from abroad, or manufactures at home. The West derives from the East supplies requisite to its growth and comfort, and, what is perhaps of still greater consequence, it must of necessity owe the secure enjoyment of indispensable outlets for its own productions to the weight, influence, and the future maritime strength of the Atlantic side of the Union, directed by an indissoluble community of interest as one nation. Any other tenure, by which the West can hold this essential advantage, whether derived from its own separate strength, or from an apostate and unnatural connection with any foreign power, must be intrinsically precarious.

While, then, every part of our country thus feels an immediate and particular interest in Union, all the parts combined cannot fail to find in the united mass of means and efforts greater strength, greater resource, proportionably greater security from external danger, a less frequent interruption of their peace by foreign nations; and, what is of inestimable value, they must derive from Union an exemption from those broils and wars between themselves, which so frequently afflict neighboring countries not tied together by the same governments, which their own rival ships alone would be sufficient to produce, but which opposite foreign alliances, attachments, and intrigues would stimulate and embitter. Hence, likewise, they will avoid the necessity of those overgrown military establishments, which, under any form of government, are inauspicious to liberty, and which are to be regarded as particularly hostile to Republican Liberty. In this sense it is, that your Union ought to be considered as a main prop of your liberty, and that the love of the one ought to endear to you the preservation of the other.

These considerations speak a persuasive language to every reflecting and virtuous mind, and exhibit the continuance of the union as a primary object of Patriotic desire. Is there a doubt, whether a common government can embrace so large a sphere? Let experience solve it. To listen to mere speculation in such a case were criminal. We are authorized to hope, that a proper organization of the whole, with the auxiliary agency of governments for the respective subdivisions, will afford a happy issue to the experiment. It is well worth a fair and full experiment. With such powerful and obvious motives to Union, affecting all parts of our country, while experience shall not have demonstrated its impracticability, there will always be reason to distrust the patriotism of those, who in any quarter may endeavor to weaken its bands.

In contemplating the causes, which may disturb our Union, it occurs as matter of serious concern, that any ground should have been furnished for characterizing parties by Geographical discriminations, Northern and Southern, Atlantic and Western; whence designing men may endeavor to excite a belief, that there is a real difference of local interests and views. One of the expedients of party to acquire influence, within particular districts, is to misrepresent the opinions and aims of other districts. You cannot shield yourselves too much against the jealousies and heart-burnings, which spring from these misrepresentations; they tend to render alien to each other those, who ought to be bound together by fraternal affection. The inhabitants of our western country have lately had a useful lesson on this head; they have seen, in the negotiation by the Executive, and in the unanimous ratification by the Senate, of the treaty with Spain, and in the universal satisfaction at that event, throughout the United States, a decisive proof how unfounded were the suspicions propagated among them of a policy in the General Government and in the Atlantic States unfriendly to their interests in regard to the Mississippi; they have been witnesses to the formation of two treaties, that with Great Britain, and that with Spain, which secure to them everything they could desire, in respect to our foreign relations, towards confirming their prosperity. Will it not be their wisdom to rely for the preservation of these advantages on the union by which they were procured? Will they not henceforth be deaf to those advisers, if such there are, who would sever them from their brethren, and connect them with aliens?

To the efficacy and permanency of your Union, a Government for the whole is indispensable. No alliances, however strict, between the parts can be an adequate substitute; they must inevitably experience the infractions and interruptions, which all alliances in all times have experienced. Sensible of this momentous truth, you have improved upon your first essay, by the adoption of a Constitution of Government better calculated than your former for an intimate Union, and for the efficacious management of your common concerns. This Government, the offspring of our own choice, uninfluenced and unawed, adopted upon full investigation and mature deliberation, completely free in its principles, in the distribution of its powers, uniting security with energy, and containing within itself a provision for its own amendment, has a just claim to your confidence and your support. Respect for its authority, compliance with its laws, acquiescence in its measures, are duties enjoined by the fundamental maxims of true Liberty. The basis of our political systems is the right of the people to make and to alter their Constitutions of Government. But the Constitution which at any time exists, till changed by an explicit and authentic act of the whole people, is sacredly obligatory upon all. The very idea of the power and the right of the people to establish Government presupposes the duty of every individual to obey the established Government.

All obstructions to the execution of the Laws, all combinations and associations, under whatever plausible character, with the real design to direct, control, counteract, or awe the regular deliberation and action of the constituted authorities, are destructive of this fundamental principle, and of fatal tendency. They serve to organize faction, to give it an artificial and extraordinary force; to put, in the place of the delegated will of the nation, the will of a party, often a small but artful and enterprising minority of the community; and, according to the alternate triumphs of different parties, to make the public administration the mirror of the ill-concerted and incongruous projects of faction, rather than the organ of consistent and wholesome plans digested by common counsels, and modified by mutual interests.

However combinations or associations of the above description may now and then answer popular ends, they are likely, in the course of time and things, to become potent engines, by which cunning, ambitious, and unprincipled men will be enabled to subvert the power of the people, and to usurp for themselves the reins of government; destroying afterwards the very engines, which have lifted them to unjust dominion.

Towards the preservation of your government, and the permanency of your present happy state, it is requisite, not only that you steadily discountenance irregular oppositions to its acknowledged authority, but also that you resist with care the spirit of innovation upon its principles, however specious the pretexts. One method of assault may be to effect, in the forms of the constitution, alterations, which will impair the energy of the system, and thus to undermine what cannot be directly overthrown. In all the changes to which you may be invited, remember that time and habit are at least as necessary to fix the true character of governments, as of other human institutions; that experience is the surest standard, by which to test the real tendency of the existing constitution of a country; that facility in changes, upon the credit of mere hypothesis and opinion, exposes to perpetual change, from the endless variety of hypothesis and opinion; and remember, especially, that, for the efficient management of our common interests, in a country so extensive as ours, a government of as much vigor as is consistent with the perfect security of liberty is indispensable. Liberty itself will find in such a government, with powers properly distributed and adjusted, its surest guardian. It is, indeed, little else than a name, where the government is too feeble to withstand the enterprises of faction, to confine each member of the society within the limits prescribed by the laws, and to maintain all in the secure and tranquil enjoyment of the rights of person and property.

I have already intimated to you the danger of parties in the state, with particular reference to the founding of them on geographical discriminations. Let me now take a more comprehensive view, and warn you in the most solemn manner against the baneful effects of the spirit of party, generally.

This spirit, unfortunately, is inseparable from our nature, having its root in the strongest passions of the human mind. It exists under different shapes in all governments, more or less stifled, controlled, or repressed; but, in those of the popular form, it is seen in its greatest rankness, and is truly their worst enemy.

The alternate domination of one faction over another, sharpened by the spirit of revenge, natural to party dissension, which in different ages and countries has perpetrated the most horrid enormities, is itself a frightful despotism. But this leads at length to a more formal and permanent despotism. The disorders and miseries, which result, gradually incline the minds of men to seek security and repose in the absolute power of an individual; and sooner or later the chief of some prevailing faction, more able or more fortunate than his competitors, turns this disposition to the purposes of his own elevation, on the ruins of Public Liberty.

Without looking forward to an extremity of this kind, (which nevertheless ought not to be entirely out of sight,) the common and continual mischiefs of the spirit of party are sufficient to make it the interest and duty of a wise people to discourage and restrain it.

It serves always to distract the Public Councils, and enfeeble the Public Administration. It agitates the Community with ill-founded jealousies and false alarms; kindles the animosity of one part against another, foments occasionally riot and insurrection. It opens the door to foreign influence and corruption, which find a facilitated access to the government itself through the channels of party passions. Thus the policy and the will of one country are subjected to the policy and will of another.

There is an opinion, that parties in free countries are useful checks upon the administration of the Government, and serve to keep alive the spirit of Liberty. This within certain limits is probably true; and in Governments of a Monarchical cast, Patriotism may look with indulgence, if not with favor, upon the spirit of party. But in those of the popular character, in Governments purely elective, it is a spirit not to be encouraged. From their natural tendency, it is certain there will always be enough of that spirit for every salutary purpose. And, there being constant danger of excess, the effort ought to be, by force of public opinion, to mitigate and assuage it. A fire not to be quenched, it demands a uniform vigilance to prevent its bursting into a flame, lest, instead of warming, it should consume.

It is important, likewise, that the habits of thinking in a free country should inspire caution, in those in-trusted with its administration, to confine themselves within their respective constitutional spheres, avoiding in the exercise of the powers of one department to encroach upon another. The spirit of encroachment tends to consolidate the powers of all the departments in one, and thus to create, whatever the form of government, a real despotism. A just estimate of that love of power, and proneness to abuse it, which predominates in the human heart, is sufficient to satisfy us of the truth of this position. The necessity of reciprocal checks in the exercise of political power, by dividing and distributing it into different depositories, and constituting each the Guardian of the Public Weal against invasions by the others, has been evinced by experiments ancient and modern; some of them in our country and under our own eyes. To preserve them must be as necessary as to institute them. If, in the opinion of the people, the distribution or modification of the constitutional powers be in any particular wrong, let it be corrected by an amendment in the way, which the constitution designates. But let there be no change by usurpation; for, though this, in one instance, may be the instrument of good, it is the customary weapon by which free governments are destroyed. The precedent must always greatly overbalance in permanent evil any partial or transient benefit, which the use can at any time yield.

Of all the dispositions and habits, which lead to political prosperity, Religion and Morality are indispensable supports. In vain would that man claim the tribute of Patriotism, who should labor to subvert these great pillars of human happiness, these firmest props of the duties of Men and Citizens? The mere Politician, equally with the pious man, ought to respect and to cherish them. A volume could not trace all their connections with private and public felicity. Let it simply be asked, where is the security for property, for reputation, for life, if the sense of religious obligation desert the oaths, which are the instruments of investigation in Courts of Justice? And let us with caution indulge the supposition, that morality can be maintained without religion. Whatever may be conceded to the influence of refined education on minds of peculiar structure, reason and experience both forbid us to expect, that national morality can prevail in exclusion of religious principle.

It is substantially true, that virtue or morality is a necessary spring of popular government. The rule, indeed, extends with more or less force to every species of free government. Who, that is a sincere friend to it, can look with indifference upon attempts to shake the foundation of the fabric?

Promote, then, as an object of primary importance, institutions for the general diffusion of knowledge. In proportion as the structure of a government gives force to public opinion, it is essential that public opinion should be enlightened.

As a very important source of strength and security, cherish public credit. One method of preserving it is, to use it as sparingly as possible; avoiding occasions of expense by cultivating peace, but remembering also that timely disbursements to prepare for danger frequently prevent much greater disbursements to repel it; avoiding likewise the accumulation of debt, not only by shunning occasions of expense, but by vigorous exertions in time of peace to discharge the debts, which unavoidable wars may have occasioned, not ungenerously throwing upon posterity the burthen, which we ourselves ought to bear. The execution of these maxims belongs to your representatives, but it is necessary that public opinion should cooperate. To facilitate to them the performance of their duty, it is essential that you should practically bear in mind, that towards the payment of debts there must be Revenue; that to have Revenue there must be taxes; that no taxes can be devised, which are not more or less inconvenient and unpleasant; that the intrinsic embarrassment, inseparable from the selection of the proper objects (which is always a choice of difficulties), ought to be a decisive motive for a candid construction of the conduct of the government in making it, and for a spirit of acquiescence in the measures for obtaining revenue, which the public exigencies may at any time dictate.

Observe good faith and justice towards all Nations; cultivate peace and harmony with all. Religion and Morality enjoin this conduct; and can it be, that good policy does not equally enjoin it? It will be worthy of a free, enlightened, and, at no distant period, a great Nation, to give to mankind the magnanimous and too novel example of a people always guided by an exalted justice and benevolence. Who can doubt, that, in the course of time and things, the fruits of such a plan would richly repay any temporary advantages, which might be lost by a steady adherence to it? Can it be, that Providence has not connected the permanent felicity of a Nation with its Virtue? The experiment, at least, is recommended by every sentiment which ennobles human nature. Alas! Is it rendered impossible by its vices?

In the execution of such a plan, nothing is more essential, than that permanent, inveterate antipathies against particular Nations, and passionate attachments for others, should be excluded; and that, in place of them, just and amicable feelings towards all should be cultivated. The Nation, which indulges towards another an habitual hatred, or an habitual fondness, is in some degree a slave. It is a slave to its animosity or to its affection, either of which is sufficient to lead it astray from its duty and its interest. Antipathy in one nation against another disposes each more readily to offer insult and injury, to lay hold of slight causes of umbrage, and to be haughty and intractable, when accidental or trifling occasions of dispute occur. Hence frequent collisions, obstinate, envenomed, and bloody contests. The Nation, prompted by ill-will and resentment, sometimes impels to war the Government, contrary to the best calculations of policy. The Government sometimes participates in the national propensity, and adopts through passion what reason would reject; at other times, it makes the animosity of the nation subservient to projects of hostility instigated by pride, ambition, and other sinister and pernicious motives. The peace often, sometimes perhaps the liberty, of Nations has been the victim.

So likewise, a passionate attachment of one Nation for another produces a variety of evils. Sympathy for the favorite Nation, facilitating the illusion of an imaginary common interest, in cases where no real common interest exists, and infusing into one the enmities of the other, betrays the former into a participation in the quarrels and wars of the latter, without adequate inducement or justification. It leads also to concessions to the favorite Nation of privileges denied to others, which is apt doubly to injure the Nation making the concessions; by unnecessarily parting with what ought to have been retained; and by exciting jealousy, ill-will, and a disposition to retaliate, in the parties from whom equal privileges are withheld. And it gives to ambitious, corrupted, or deluded citizens, (who devote themselves to the favorite nation,) facility to betray or sacrifice the interests of their own country, without odium, sometimes even with popularity; gilding, with the appearances of a virtuous sense of obligation, a commendable deference for public opinion, or a laudable zeal for public good, the base or foolish compliances of ambition, corruption, or infatuation.

As avenues to foreign influence in innumerable ways, such attachments are particularly alarming to the truly enlightened and independent Patriot. How many opportunities do they afford to tamper with domestic factions, to practice the arts of seduction, to mislead public opinion, to influence or awe the

Public Councils! Such an attachment of a small or weak, towards a great and powerful nation, dooms the former to be the satellite of the latter.

Against the insidious wiles of foreign influence (I conjure you to believe me, fellow-citizens,) the jealousy of a free people ought to be constantly awake; since history and experience prove, that foreign influence is one of the most baneful foes of Republican Government. But that jealousy, to be useful, must be impartial; else it becomes the instrument of the very influence to be avoided, instead of a defense against it. Excessive partiality for one foreign nation, and excessive dislike of another, cause those whom they actuate to see danger only on one side, and serve to veil and even second the arts of influence on the other. Real patriots, who may resist the intrigues of the favorite, are liable to become suspected and odious; while its tools and dupes usurp the applause and confidence of the people, to surrender their interests.

The great rule of conduct for us, in regard to foreign nations, is, in extending our commercial relations, to have with them as little political connections as possible. So far as we have already formed engagements, let them be fulfilled with perfect good faith. Here let us stop.

Europe has a set of primary interests, which to us have none, or a very remote relation. Hence she must be engaged in frequent controversies, the causes of which are essentially foreign to our concerns. Hence, therefore, it must be unwise in us to implicate ourselves, by artificial ties, in the ordinary vicissitudes of her politics, or the ordinary combinations and collisions of her friendships or enmities.

Our detached and distant situation invites and enables us to pursue a different course. If we remain one people, under an efficient government, the period is not far off, when we may defy material injury from external annoyance; when we may take such an attitude as will cause the neutrality, we may at any time resolve upon, to be scrupulously respected; when belligerent nations, under the impossibility of making acquisitions upon us, will not lightly hazard the giving us provocation; when we may choose peace or war, as our interest, guided by justice, shall counsel.

Why forego the advantages of so peculiar a situation? Why quit our own to stand upon foreign ground? Why, by interweaving our destiny with that of any part of Europe, entangle our peace and prosperity in the toils of European ambition, rival ship, interest, humor, or caprice?

It is our true policy to steer clear of permanent alliances with any portion of the foreign world; so far, I mean, as we are now at liberty to do it; for let me not be understood as capable of patronizing infidelity to existing engagements. I hold the maxim no less applicable to public than to private affairs, that honesty is always the best policy. I repeat it, therefore, let those engagements be observed in their genuine sense. But, in my opinion, it is unnecessary and would be unwise to extend them.

Taking care always to keep ourselves, by suitable establishments, on a respectable defensive posture, we may safely trust to temporary alliances for extraordinary emergencies.

Harmony, liberal intercourse with all nations, are recommended by policy, humanity, and interest. But even our commercial policy should hold an equal and impartial hand; neither seeking nor granting exclusive favors or preferences; consulting the natural course of things; diffusing and diversifying by gentle means the streams of commerce, but forcing nothing; establishing, with powers so disposed, in order to give trade a stable course, to define the rights of our merchants, and to enable the government to support them, conventional rules of intercourse, the best that present circumstances and mutual opinion will permit, but temporary, and liable to be from time to time abandoned or varied, as experience and circumstances shall dictate; constantly keeping in view, that it is folly in one nation to look for disinterested favors from another; that it must pay with a portion of its independence for whatever it may accept under that character; that, by such acceptance, it may place itself in the condition of having given equivalents for nominal favors, and yet of being reproached with ingratitude for not giving more. There can be no greater error than to expect or calculate upon real favors from nation to nation. It is an illusion, which experience must cure, which a just pride ought to discard.

In offering to you, my countrymen, these counsels of an old and affectionate friend, I dare not hope they will make the strong and lasting impression I could wish; that they will control the usual current of the passions, or prevent our nation from running the course, which has hitherto marked the destiny of nations. But, if I may even flatter myself, that they may be productive of some partial benefit, some occasional good; that they may now and then recur to moderate the fury of party spirit, to warn against the mischiefs of foreign intrigue, to guard against the impostures of pretended patriotism; this hope will be a full recompense for the solicitude for your welfare, by which they have been dictated.

How far in the discharge of my official duties, I have been guided by the principles which have been delineated, the public records and other evidences of my conduct must witness to you and to the world. To myself, the assurance of my own conscience is, that I have at least believed myself to be guided by them.

In relation to the still subsisting war in Europe, my

Proclamation of the 22d of April 1793 is the index to my Plan. Sanctioned by your approving voice, and by that of your Representatives in both Houses of Congress, the spirit of that measure has continually governed me, uninfluenced by any attempts to deter or divert me from it.

After deliberate examination, with the aid of the best lights I could obtain, I was well satisfied that our country, under all the circumstances of the case, had a right to take, and was bound in duty and interest to take, a neutral position. Having taken it, I determined, as far as should depend upon me, to maintain it, with moderation, perseverance, and firmness.

The considerations, which respect the right to hold this conduct, it is not necessary on this occasion to detail. I will only observe, that, according to my understanding of the matter, that right, so far from being denied by any of the Belligerent Powers, has been virtually admitted by all.

The duty of holding a neutral conduct may be inferred, without anything more, from the obligation which justice and humanity impose on every nation, in cases in which it is free to act, to maintain inviolate the relations of peace and amity towards other nations.

The inducements of interest for observing that conduct will best be referred to your own reflections and experience. With me, a predominant motive has been to endeavor to gain time to our country to settle and mature its yet recent institutions, and to progress without interruption to that degree of strength and consistency, which is necessary to give it, humanly speaking, the command of its own fortunes.

Though, in reviewing the incidents of my administration, I am unconscious of intentional error, I am nevertheless too sensible of my defects not to think it probable that I may have committed many errors. Whatever they may be, I fervently beseech the Almighty to avert or mitigate the evils to which they may tend. I shall also carry with me the hope, that my Country will never cease to view them with indulgence; and that, after forty-five years of my life dedicated to its service with an upright zeal, the faults of incompetent abilities will be consigned to oblivion, as myself must soon be to the mansions of rest.

Relying on its kindness in this as in other things, and actuated by that fervent love towards it, which is so natural to a man, who views it in the native soil of himself and his progenitors for several generations; I anticipate with pleasing expectation that retreat, in which I promise myself to realize, without alloy, the sweet enjoyment of partaking, in the midst of my fellow-citizens, the benign influence of good laws under a free government, the ever favorite object of my heart, and the happy reward, as I trust, of our mutual cares, labors, and dangers.

First Inaugural Address of Franklin D. Roosevelt

March 4, 1933

President Hoover, Mr. Chief Justice, my friends:

This is a day of national consecration. And I am certain that on this day my fellow Americans expect that on my induction into the Presidency, I will address them with a candor and a decision which the present situation of our people impels.

This is preeminently the time to speak the truth, the whole truth, frankly and boldly. Nor need we shrink from honestly facing conditions in our country today. This great Nation will endure, as it has endured, will revive and will prosper.

So, first of all, let me assert my firm belief that the only thing we have to fear is fear itself — nameless, unreasoning, unjustified terror which paralyzes needed efforts to convert retreat into advance. In every dark hour of our national life, a leadership of frankness and of vigor has met with that understanding and support of the people themselves which is essential to victory. And I am convinced that you will again give that support to leadership in these critical days.

In such a spirit on my part and on yours we face our common difficulties. They concern, thank God, only material things. Values have shrunk to fantastic levels; taxes have risen; our ability to pay has fallen; government of all kinds is faced by serious curtailment of income; the means of exchange are frozen in the currents of trade; the withered leaves of industrial enterprise lie on every side; farmers find no markets for their produce; and the savings of many years in thousands of families are gone. More important, a host of unemployed citizens face the grim problem of existence and an equally great number toil with little return. Only a foolish optimist can deny the dark realities of the moment.

And yet our distress comes from no failure of substance. We are stricken by no plague of locusts. Compared with the perils which our forefathers conquered, because they believed and were not afraid, we have still much to be thankful for. Nature still offers her bounty and human efforts have multiplied it. Plenty is at our doorstep, but a generous use of it languishes in the very sight of the supply.

Primarily, this is because the rulers of the exchange of mankind's goods have failed, through their own stubbornness and their own incompetence, have admitted their failure, and have abdicated. Practices of the unscrupulous money changers stand indicted in the court of public opinion, rejected by the hearts and minds of men.

True, they have tried. But their efforts have been cast in the pattern of an outworn tradition. Faced by failure of credit, they have proposed only the lending of more money. Stripped of the lure of profit by which to induce our people to follow their false leadership, they have resorted to exhortations, pleading tearfully for restored confidence. They only know the rules of a generation of self-seekers. They have no vision, and when there is no vision the people perish.

Yes, the money changers have fled from their high seats in the temple of our civilization. We may now restore that temple to the ancient truths. The measure of that restoration lies in the extent to which we apply social values more noble than mere monetary profit.

Happiness lies not in the mere possession of money; it lies in the joy of achievement, in the thrill of creative effort. The joy, the moral stimulation of work no longer must be forgotten in the mad chase of evanescent profits. These dark days, my friends, will be worth all they cost us if they teach us that our true destiny is not to be ministered unto but to minister to ourselves, to our fellow men.

Recognition of that falsity of material wealth as the standard of success goes hand in hand with the abandonment of the false belief that public office and high political position are to be valued only by the standards of pride of place and personal profit; and there must be an end to a conduct in banking and in business which too often has given to a sacred trust the likeness of callous and selfish wrongdoing. Small wonder that confidence languishes, for it thrives only on honesty, on honor, on the sacredness of obligations, on faithful protection, and on unselfish performance; without them it cannot live.

Restoration calls, however, not for changes in ethics alone. This Nation is asking for action, and action now.

Our greatest primary task is to put people to work. This is no unsolvable problem if we face it wisely and courageously. It can be accomplished in part by direct recruiting by the Government itself, treating the task as we would treat the emergency of a war, but at the same time, through this employment, accomplishing great — greatly needed projects to stimulate and reorganize the use of our great natural resources.

Hand in hand with that we must frankly recognize the overbalance of population in our industrial centers and, by engaging on a national scale in redistribution, endeavor to provide a better use of the land for those best fitted for the land.

Yes, the task can be helped by definite efforts to raise the values of agricultural products, and with this the power to purchase the output of our cities. It can be helped by preventing realistically the tragedy of the growing loss through foreclosure of our small homes and our farms. It can be helped by insistence that the Federal, the State, and the local governments act forthwith on the demand that their cost be drastically reduced. It can be helped by the unifying of relief activities which today are often scattered, uneconomical, unequal. It can be helped by national planning for and supervision of all forms of transportation and of communications and other utilities that have a definitely public character. There are many ways in which it can be helped, but it can never be helped by merely talking about it.

We must act. We must act quickly.

And finally, in our progress towards a resumption of work, we require two safeguards against a return of the evils of the old order. There must be a strict supervision of all banking and credits and investments. There must be an end to speculation with other people's money. And there must be provision for an adequate but sound currency.

These, my friends, are the lines of attack. I shall presently urge upon a new Congress in special session detailed measures for their fulfillment, and I shall seek the immediate assistance of the 48 States.

Through this program of action we address ourselves to putting our own national house in order and making income balance outgo. Our international trade relations, though vastly important, are in point of time, and necessity, secondary to the establishment of a sound national economy. I favor, as a practical policy, the putting of first things first. I shall spare no effort to restore world trade by international economic readjustment; but the emergency at home cannot wait on that accomplishment.

The basic thought that guides these specific means of national recovery is not nationally — narrowly nationalistic. It is the insistence, as a first consideration, upon the interdependence of the various elements in and parts of the United States of America — a recognition of the old and permanently important manifestation of the American spirit of the pioneer. It is the way to recovery. It is the immediate way. It is the strongest assurance that recovery will endure.

In the field of world policy, I would dedicate this Nation to the policy of the good neighbor: the neighbor who resolutely respects himself and, because he does so, respects the rights of others; the neighbor who respects his obligations and respects the sanctity of his agreements in and with a world of neighbors.

If I read the temper of our people correctly, we now realize, as we have never realized before, our interdependence on each other; that we cannot merely take, but we must give as well; that if we are to go forward, we must move as a trained and loyal army willing to sacrifice for the good of a common discipline, because without such discipline no progress can be made, no leadership becomes effective.

We are, I know, ready and willing to submit our lives and our property to such discipline, because it makes possible a leadership which aims at the larger good. This, I propose to offer, pledging that the larger purposes will bind upon us, bind upon us all as a sacred obligation with a unity of duty hitherto evoked only in times of armed strife.

With this pledge taken, I assume unhesitatingly the leadership of this great army of our people dedicated to a disciplined attack upon our common problems.

Action in this image, action to this end is feasible under the form of government which we have inherited from our ancestors. Our Constitution is so simple, so practical that it is possible always to meet extraordinary needs by changes in emphasis and arrangement without loss of essential form. That is why our constitutional system has proved itself the most superbly enduring political mechanism the modern world has ever seen.

It has met every stress of vast expansion of territory, of foreign wars, of bitter internal strife, of world relations. And it is to be hoped that the normal balance of executive and legislative authority may be wholly equal, wholly adequate to meet the unprecedented task before us. But it may be that an unprecedented demand and need for undelayed action may call for temporary departure from that normal balance of public procedure.

I am prepared under my constitutional duty to recommend the measures that a stricken nation in the midst of a stricken world may require. These measures, or such other measures as the Congress may build out of its experience and wisdom, I shall seek, within my constitutional authority, to bring to speedy adoption.

But, in the event that the Congress shall fail to take one of these two courses, in the event that the national emergency is still critical, I shall not evade the clear course of duty that will then confront me. I shall ask the Congress for the one remaining instrument to meet the crisis — broad Executive power to wage a war against the emergency, as great as the power that would be given to me if we were in fact invaded by a foreign foe.

For the trust reposed in me, I will return the courage and the devotion that befit the time. I can do no less.

We face the arduous days that lie before us in the warm courage of national unity; with the clear consciousness of seeking old and precious moral values; with the clean satisfaction that comes from the stern performance of duty by old and young alike. We aim at the assurance of a rounded, a permanent national life.

We do not distrust the — the future of essential democracy. The people of the United States have not failed. In their need they have registered a mandate that they want direct, vigorous action. They have asked for discipline and direction under leadership. They have made me the present instrument of their wishes. In the spirit of the gift I take it.

In this dedication — in this dedication of a Nation, we humbly ask the blessing of God.

May He protect each and every one of us.

May He guide me in the days to come.

Inaugural Address of
John F. Kennedy

January 20, 1961

Vice President Johnson, Mr. Speaker, Mr. Chief Justice, President Eisenhower, Vice President Nixon, President Truman, reverend clergy, fellow citizens:

We observe today not a victory of party, but a celebration of freedom — symbolizing an end, as well as a beginning — signifying renewal, as well as change. For I have sworn before you and Almighty God the same solemn oath our forebears prescribed nearly a century and three-quarters ago.

The world is very different now. For man holds in his mortal hands the power to abolish all forms of human poverty and all forms of human life. And yet the same revolutionary beliefs for which our forebears fought are still at issue around the globe — the belief that the rights of man come not from the generosity of the state, but from the hand of God.

We dare not forget today that we are the heirs of that first revolution. Let the word go forth from this time and place, to friend and foe alike, that the torch has been passed to a new generation of Americans — born in this century, tempered by war, disciplined by a hard and bitter peace, proud of our ancient heritage, and unwilling to witness or permit the slow undoing of those human rights to which this nation has always been committed, and to which we are committed today at home and around the world.

Let every nation know, whether it wishes us well or ill, that we shall pay any price, bear any burden, meet any hardship, support any friend, oppose any foe, to assure the survival and the success of liberty.

This much we pledge — and more.

To those old allies whose cultural and spiritual origins we share, we pledge the loyalty of faithful friends. United there is little we cannot do in a host of cooperative ventures. Divided there is little we can do — for we dare not meet a powerful challenge at odds and split as under.

To those new states whom we welcome to the ranks of the free, we pledge our word that one form of colonial control shall not have passed away merely to be replaced by a far more iron tyranny. We shall not always expect to find them supporting our view. But we shall always hope to find them strongly supporting their own freedom — and to remember that, in the past, those who foolishly sought power by riding the back of the tiger ended up inside.

To those people in the huts and villages of half the globe struggling to break the bonds of mass misery, we pledge our best efforts to help them help themselves, for whatever period is required — not because the Communists may be doing it, not because we seek their votes, but because it is right. If a free society cannot help the many who are poor, it cannot save the few who are rich.

To our sister republics south of our border, we offer a special pledge: to convert our good words into good deeds, in a new alliance for progress, to assist free men and free governments in casting off the chains of poverty. But this peaceful revolution of hope cannot become the prey of hostile powers. Let all our neighbors know that we shall join with them to oppose aggression or subversion anywhere in the Americas. And let every other power know that this hemisphere intends to remain the master of its own house.

To that world assembly of sovereign states, the United Nations, our last best hope in an age where the instruments of war have far outpaced the instruments of peace, we renew our pledge of support — to prevent it from becoming merely a forum for invective, to strengthen its shield of the new and the weak, and to enlarge the area in which its writ may run.

Finally, to those nations who would make themselves our adversary, we offer not a pledge but a request: that both sides begin anew the quest for peace, before the dark powers of destruction unleashed by science engulf all humanity in planned or accidental self-destruction.

We dare not tempt them with weakness. For only when our arms are sufficient beyond doubt can we be certain beyond doubt that they will never be employed.

But neither can two great and powerful groups of nations take comfort from our present course — both sides overburdened by the cost of modern weapons, both rightly alarmed by the steady spread of the deadly atom, yet both racing to alter that uncertain balance of terror that stays the hand of mankind's final war.

So let us begin anew — remembering on both sides that civility is not a sign of weakness, and sincerity is always subject to proof. Let us never negotiate out of fear, but let us never fear to negotiate.

Let both sides explore what problems unite us instead of belaboring those problems which divide us.

Let both sides, for the first time, formulate serious and precise proposals for the inspection and control of arms, and bring the absolute power to destroy other nations under the absolute control of all nations.

Let both sides seek to invoke the wonders of science instead of its terrors. Together let us explore the stars, conquer the deserts, eradicate disease, tap the ocean depths, and encourage the arts and commerce.

Let both sides unite to heed, in all corners of the earth, the command of Isaiah — to "undo the heavy burdens, and to let the oppressed go free."

And, if a beachhead of cooperation may push back the jungle of suspicion, let both sides join in creating a new endeavor — not a new balance of power, but a new world of law — where the strong are just, and the weak secure, and the peace preserved.

All this will not be finished in the first one hundred days. Nor will it be finished in the first one thousand days; nor in the life of this Administration; nor even perhaps in our lifetime on this planet. But let us begin.

In your hands, my fellow citizens, more than mine, will rest the final success or failure of our course. Since this country was founded, each generation of Americans has been summoned to give testimony to its national loyalty. The graves of young Americans who answered the call to service surround the globe.

Now the trumpet summons us again — not as a call to bear arms, though arms we need — not as a call to battle, though embattled we are — but a call to bear the burden of a long twilight struggle, year in and year out, "rejoicing in hope; patient in tribulation," a struggle against the common enemies of man: tyranny, poverty, disease, and war itself.

Can we forge against these enemies a grand and global alliance, North and South, East and West, that can assure a more fruitful life for all mankind? Will you join in that historic effort?

In the long history of the world, only a few generations have been granted the role of defending freedom in its hour of maximum danger. I do not shrink from this responsibility — I welcome it. I do not believe that any of us would exchange places with any other people or any other generation. The energy, the faith, the devotion which we bring to this endeavor will light our country and all who serve it. And the glow from that fire can truly light the world.

And so, my fellow Americans, ask not what your country can do for you; ask what you can do for your country.

My fellow citizens of the world, ask not what America will do for you, but what together we can do for the freedom of man.

Finally, whether you are citizens of America or citizens of the world, ask of us here the same high standards of strength and sacrifice which we ask of you. With a good conscience our only sure reward, with history the final judge of our deeds, let us go forth to lead the land we love, asking His blessing and His help, but knowing that here on earth God's work must truly be our own.

Abraham Lincoln's Gettysburg Address

1863

Four score and seven years ago our fathers brought forth, upon this continent, a new nation, conceived in Liberty, and dedicated to the proposition that all men are created equal.

Now we are engaged in a great civil war, testing whether that nation, or any nation so conceived, and so dedicated, can long endure. We are met here on a great battlefield of that war. We have come to dedicate a portion of it as a final resting place for those who here gave their lives that that nation might live. It is altogether fitting and proper that we should do this.

But in a larger sense we cannot dedicate – we cannot consecrate – we cannot hallow this ground. The brave men, living and dead, who struggled, here, have consecrated it far above our poor power to add or detract. The world will little note, nor long remember, what we say here, but can never forget what they did here.

It is for us, the living, rather to be dedicated here to the unfinished work which they have, thus far, so nobly carried on. It is rather for us to be here dedicated to the great task remaining before us – that from these honored dead we take increased devotion to that cause for which they here gave the last full measure of devotion – that we here highly resolve that these dead shall not have died in vain; that this nation shall have a new birth of freedom; and that this government of the people, by the people, for the people, shall not perish from the earth.

...

The thirteen speeches listed above portray many important concepts: patriotism, conviction, effective public speaking, strong leadership and great vision. If you study and truly understand how and why these public figures said what they said and when they said it, you will begin to understand what American patriotism, effective communication and leadership are all about. And these three concepts will lead you to a very successful and fulfilled life.

Chapter 7

Developing Your Foundation

"Intellectual growth should commence at
birth and cease at death."
—Albert Einstein

Accept the Things You Cannot Change and the Courage to Change the Things You Can, and the Wisdom to Know the Difference -

If we can accept and embrace the things we cannot change, and instead work on changing ourselves, we could capitalize on our situation and change our lives for the better. You can control your destiny and gain all those benefits life has to offer. It doesn't mean you are a failure, because you aren't where you want to be in your life right now; if you want a better life (you would not be reading this book if you didn't), you'll have to spend the energy to change yourself; to read the books, to be around people who can move you, and help you get where you want to be. Then the world will change for you, because you have changed.

Many years ago I said to a friend of mine, "You can't have an ego in the journey to success." My friend did not comprehend this concept; he was one of those people who felt they knew everything. He didn't study when he was supposed to; he blamed others when he didn't succeed. He couldn't understand why he failed; it never occurred to him that his ego was not allowing him to succeed. Humility is the key: To know what we do not know.

The "ego philosophy" is very simple. Put your ego in your back pocket when it comes to the journey of success. Later you can take a little ego out and put it in front of you, because you need a little ego to carry you forward, but not all your ego. Do not think you know it all, always be open to new ideas and learning new things. You need to learn more so you can become more.

Top leaders are never finished learning. Do you think because you have two hundred grand in the bank that you would want to stop there, and not earn anymore? Success is a journey and not a destination, success will put you in touch with who you are, it will put you in places that you can't see right now, when you get there you will realize that the process of getting there is more important than arriving. That's why successful people keep striving: it keeps them growing. It's that simple.

People who are not doing well financially try to give advice about business. I don't listen to them, I'm polite, I don't listen. I had a sales executive that left her position with our company, and was not doing well at her new company, and although she said she liked sales and wanted to succeed, she wouldn't cold call and do what it takes to succeed in sales. What astounded me was she called six months later and said, "Randy, I have a wonderful opportunity and I want to share it with you." This same woman who had not succeeded in my sales organization was now trying to entice me into going with her to a new company.

DEVELOPING YOUR FOUNDATION   187

Someone had deluded her into believing that she could succeed without changing her FOUNDATION. This unsuccessful sales executive wanted me to enter into a business partnership with her and her husband, I listened. They had a used BMW, they had a Rolex that they were probably paying on with installments, they lived in an area that could be considered upscale, they were an attractive couple, but were trying to delude others that they had made it. They were definitely "Faking it, until they made it."

Her FOUNDATION was no different then when she failed with my organization. I needed to give this couple some advice; I saw very clearly where they were going wrong. I said, "Listen, you're a wonderful couple, let me give you something that you can take back with you to change your life, because I can tell you both want to succeed in life: "You have to develop a stronger FOUNDATION than what you have."

You're coming to me, because you think that I can make you a lot of money, what do you have to offer me?" He said, "An opportunity we're involved with." When I asked him if they succeeded yet, he said, "Well no, we're just getting started." And I said, "Well, I don't want to bust your bubble, you're excited, and that's okay, but chances are a year from now you won't be in the same business."

A year later, guess what? They're not in the business, because it just didn't work out for them, why didn't it work out, because they're not who they said they were. If you have a really solid FOUNDATION, you're going to make it, and it does not matter what business it is. If you change your job before you change your FOUNDATION, it's not going to work, it's that simple. This couple had not changed their work ethic, so they were destined to fail regardless of the opportunity.

There are many aspects to a solid FOUNDATION: spiritual, family, physical and career. When I used to interview sales people for positions throughout the country, I asked them, "What do you want to make in of income for the year?" Their comment was usually between seventy to hundred thousand a year". I was not familiar with their FOUNDATION, or their ability at that time, so I would ask them, "Why do you feel that you want to make that, and why do you feel you're worth that type of income". If the year before, they had made thirty thousand, the question would stump them.

As I wrote earlier in the book, if you want to earn more, you have got to become more, it's that simple, if you want to increase your income, you have to develop a value to the market place, it's not simply a matter of wanting it, showing up, or setting goals for it; you have to educate yourself to become more in order to earn more and give back. The action you take to achieve your goals is what will get you where you want to be in life.

Check your FOUNDATION. Are you who you say you are, are you an asset, or are you a liability to your current employer? If you think about this do you need your company more than they need you? If the answer is yes, you're in trouble. And I'll say that again, if the answer is yes, if you need your company more than they need you, folks, you're in trouble, because you have not developed any type of network that the company would want to invest in, other than having you fill in a vacancy, a territory, a seat, or an open spot. It's that simple.

Ask yourself, "What is my value?" What is my net worth from an employer's standpoint, or a customer's standpoint: if you weighed 190 pounds, would you be 190 pounds of in-shape muscle, able to pull your load, and able to carry your weight and be productive, or 190 pounds of fat taking up space. Do the action it takes to become that valuable person.

You can't beat the system. The system is going to beat you! You know down deep inside whether or not you worked hard enough to validate your current situation. If you're not maximizing your efforts, if you're not doing everything that you can do to maintain your job security, you'll be unemployed. If you think that being unemployed is easy, and that you're going to roll into another great opportunity, you've got another thing coming.

Ask yourself if what you're currently doing is moving you toward or away from the goals that you want to obtain; Again look at all areas in your life: spiritual, family, and your career, as well as your health. All are very important.

Where are you right now? Are you able to maximize what you want out of life? If the answer is "no," you might need to move on, and that's okay. But remember, the opportunity does not lie within the company, it lies within you. Look at that couple I mentioned earlier where the woman got into the multi-level program. Someone promised her the "pie in the sky," and because she was looking for the easy way out, she fell into the trap of changing the job, rather than changing her FOUNDATION and her work ethic.

Invest in yourself.

> *"Man's mind, once stretched by a new idea,*
> *never regains its original dimensions."*
> —Oliver Wendell Holmes

My favorite audience as a keynote speaker is sales people and business owners, because it's my profession. I understand it takes training to do well; what's interesting to me is how many people there are who want to try sales or start their own business. They feel that they can just step in and "wing it" until they can get the hang of it. Can you imagine approaching most professions that way? It's like a person wanting to try brain surgery. That individual might be motivated as all "get out," but without him investing the time to become properly trained, I doubt that you would volunteer to become his first patient.

To be paid well and to be competent, a doctor must invest in educating himself correctly in order to succeed. He doesn't just open an office and operate on a few people for a few weeks and hope to get the hang of it. Every profession has to qualify people by education and the more education the more reward. Put in another way the more you *learn the more you earn*.

The highest paid profession in the world is sales. Yet the vast majority of people fail, because they fail to invest time in training. I believe if you master your techniques, hone your skills, and understand human nature, you'll become a winner in your industry. I promise you. A lot of people try sales and they go at it with the approach of the "want to be" doctor. They're nervous, they're scared - join the crowd, I was too, many years ago.

DEVELOPING YOUR FOUNDATION 191

I got sick of starving and living in my car. I had to make a change. I began getting up at a reasonable hour and I started doing the things that I was supposed to be doing. It's called, "building a FOUNDATION." Would you not agree with me that if you do as your trainer asks you to do - in the company's training program – that you're going to succeed? Did they hire you to fail? Is it not to their advantage that you succeed? Absolutely! But it's amazing to me that sales people will come into a company and do the opposite of what they were trained to do. And then they blame the company for their failure. I tell executives if they are not doing well, "Harry, I'm sorry that it didn't work out for you, and I know that you tried to do it your own way, and by the way, I want to thank you, because you helped us with your "research and development" program at your own expense."

A lot of people who fail claim they don't have the time to study after work hours to improve their skills. They're the same people who don't have time to work out and stay in shape either. I'll bet you if you monitor their home activity, you'll find they have time to watch a couple of hours of television every night. Remember, you make other people money by watching television and you make nothing for yourself. One of the most nonproductive things that you can do is to sit around and watch television when you can be doing something to advance your career. Do you want to soar with the eagles, or do you want sit in your cage like the parrot. If something is truly important, you'll find the time and energy to move forward and complete the project.

Absolutely!

The challenge is there are a lot of important things we should be doing. When something is important, you make the time, make productive things your priority, prioritize important tasks by their need level and set goals to get them done.

People who talk one way and spend time doing something else are not being true to themselves, or anyone else. You have to be who you say you are because if you're not, people are going to see through you. It has to do with that internal MOTIVATION that I mentioned earlier. Have you ever been around someone who says, "Hey, have a great day," or do you have a boss who possibly has false MOTIVATIONS and tells you to keep fired up, but isn't fired up himself? You can see through false MOTIVATION. Internal MOTIVATION cannot be faked.

When I first started with the company that I was with, I had some discipline. I was in the gym every morning and I understood work ethics, somewhat. But I didn't take the same work ethic with me to work and that's why I wasn't successful. I had to strengthen my FOUNDATION in all areas of my life and internalize my MOTIVATION. I did not know it at the time, but I can look back now and see how important my FOUNDATION was for business success.

I am internally motivated, not externally motivated, I have to be, I have no choice, because I am paid for my attitude, if I rely on outside circumstances to pump me up, I will be on an emotional roller-coaster and my performance will be up and down. People don't come to hear me speak and pay good money for me to stand up and say, "Hey, I'm not going to perform 100% today, because, quite frankly, I'm a little tired," or, "I got in late last night and I'm dealing with a two-hour time change, which caused me to miss my workout."

I wouldn't be offering you much, would I? Would you possibly walk out, or tune me out. So realize that we are basically paid according to our attitude, and that is something we can control.

"Do not wish to be anything but what you are,
and try to be that perfectly."
—St. Francis De Sales

Chapter 8

Developing the Wings to Soar in America: Taking Action

"Progress always involves risk;
you can't steal second base and keep your foot on first."
—Fredrick Wilson

This great country was founded on freedom, hard work, and a determination to go for it: It's called the free enterprise system and it creates the wealth this great country has to offer you and me.

I didn't have a purpose many years ago, it was very difficult for me to get out of bed and get going when there was nothing to look forward to except the first cup of coffee in the morning; the long drive to the office, or a rejection by a negative client.

What changed me was putting things into a POSITIVE framework, it takes more energy to be POSITIVE than it does to be negative. I had to make the decision to be POSITIVE, the negatives will creep in by themselves.

When I practiced a positive attitude things changed for me, as they will for you, you will make a lot more money, have nicer friends, have better relationships, be healthier and you'll have better kids, when you decide to have a POSITIVE attitude about life.

Another way to stay motivated is to develop pride of ownership about what it is you do. Your employer's going to see a change in you, your productivity will increase, you'll start making more money. So take pride in what you do and develop your MOTIVATION internally.

Maybe you don't feel like being motivated right now, here is some advice: "*Fake it, until you make it!*" Have a zip in your walk, have a smile on your face, your employer, family and friends are going to notice and you'll become more valuable to the world and most importantly to your family.

By reading my book you have already done something that most people won't do: You're reading this because you want more out of life. Grab one or two ideas from this book to take with you so that you can increase your enjoyment of life, increase your net worth, and increase your happiness. I hope that I can help you do that; it's what I live for.

Another part of MOTIVATION is activity. Activity and effort generate results. It's interesting though, one of my sales representatives who has been with me for a long time is consistently home between the hours of two and three o'clock in the afternoon; his activity stops too soon and holds him back. I believe that if you put at least 80% of your effort into your work, you're going to achieve tremendous things.

A. L. Williams writes in his book, "All You Can Do Is All You Can Do." He states, "*You beat 50% of America by working hard. You beat another 40% of the people in America by being a person of integrity and standing for something.*" The last 10% "*is a dogfight for the free enterprise system.*"

Many people feel that just showing up, is enough. If this is our attitude, we're in trouble as a nation. It takes more than just showing up, just showing up is not good enough. When I read A. L. William's book many years ago, I thought, "Hey, if I show up, work hard, and have integrity, I'll have 90% of what this company and country has to offer....hey, count me in, I'm going for it."

I have developed a love for what I do - if you have a passion for what you do, you will be unstoppable. This country is founded on hard work, discipline, dedication, and going for it.

I sell patriotism on a day-to-day basis, because I love it. I believe in this country and that's what keeps me going. I will never let it be said that I lost an opportunity through lack of hard work. Don't lose your health through lack of hard work either, and do not lose an opportunity through lack of motivation. If it's out there, grab it. I look at it this way, "Why can't I have everything out there if this guy has it.....why can't I have it?" I know that I can, if I just work hard enough.

Years ago I always looked at people driving more expensive cars than mine. My wife and I used to drive down the street and see someone in a luxury car and we'd always wonder what that person did for a living. Have you ever done that? In other words, would you drive by a nice neighborhood and think, "Wow, what do those people do for a living?" I can tell you what they are not doing. They don't sleep in until ten or eleven o'clock in the morning and they don't stay out until one or two o'clock that evening, drinking, destroying their bodies and minds with bad things that will not move them forward in their career and in their life.

Remember, discipline weighs ounces and regret weighs tons. It's an important point: "***Discipline weighs ounces and regret weighs tons***." Think about this for a second - going back to the disciplinary statement that I mentioned. Could you imagine when your child was first born - if you put $20.00 a month or $100.00 a month into a conservative mutual fund program - where would your child stand, financially, 20 years later? The child would be very well off, but it takes discipline. Discipline is the key to MOTIVATION. If success takes hard work, discipline and integrity, you can count me in.

I hope that we can count you in, as well.

Show up and work hard, hey, is that not the premise of a successful life? Yet five million sales people are out there today and less than one million of them make a decent income. According to Charles Gibbons in his book, "Wealth without Risk," 96% of those people who retire, retire with less than $13,000.00 a year in income and, with less than $40,000.00 socked away in investments.

The late Jim Rohn (not the sports guy) was a very successful business man, speaker, and author - and taught children in the eighth grade, how to be wealthy by the time they reached forty. You can certainly have it when you want it, if you just start today.

How many of you would love to retire right now? I know I would, 200 nights a year on the road is tough. But you know, I have a passion for what I do and I love it. And let me talk about passion for a second, because it is another key to MOTIVATION.

If you truly enjoy what you do, you're going to be motivated to get it done and do very well at it. Therefore, your income is going to rise. Believing in your job is a form of integrity which, in turn, is a form of passion.

Another part of MOTIVATION and success is helping others to succeed. As Zig Ziglar puts it, *"If you help enough people get what they want, you'll get what you want."* Because, essentially, you're putting them first and yourself second; if you start putting yourself in front of people and treating them as secondary individuals, it's not going to work for you. In other words, if you chase the dollar, I truly believe you're going to lose. You have got to chase the MISSION and purpose.

Help other people become successful and you will achieve everything you desire in life.

There are several rules that I live by, and one of them is: "Positive affirmation without discipline often leads to delusion." You see if you're POSITIVE you'll succeed at whatever it is that you discipline yourself to do. But not just through affirmations, you must take action.

Would you recognize an opportunity if it was standing right in front of: If you have an opportunity, never lose it for the lack of hard work. That is also part of my foundation. Good positions are like stock. Your stock broker calls you up and says, "Hey, I want you to invest in a particular stock." You still have to EVALUATE whether or not it's a good opportunity. Now that seems obvious, but so many people only EVALUATE the opportunity in their job when they're first hired. You need to set your goals and then see if your current opportunity allows you to meet what you set. That is what I call, "waking up."

Many years ago one of my goals was to own a brand new sports car. I got it and I worked hard for it. It was a beautiful candy-apple red. I'm not bragging about it, I just want you to know that you can go after luxury cars like I did. It's out there for you.

I probably had about 200 miles on the car and I decided go for a drive down to Tucson, Arizona. I got up at 6:00 a.m. in the morning and went out to the front of the hotel where I left the car parked the night before with the top off and the windows rolled up. I noticed that there was a stain on the side of my window. Some jealous individual had thrown a large coffee with cream inside my brand new sports car. A business owner at the time, who I had known, was watching me trying to clean the mess up. He said, "Randy, isn't it amazing how jealous some people can be?" And I said, "Yeah, Bill, you're right," but if this person would just work as hard as I do, and put the time and effort into whatever it is they're doing, he or she could probably have a sports car like this as well."

It took me five years to get out of high school. I'm no one special. I just show up and work hard, and that doesn't take a lot of brains, does it?

There are twenty-four hours in a day, and I recommend that you only work half a day - whether it's the first twelve hours or the second twelve hours - it's entirely up to you. If I can get you to maximize your output, you'll do very well at whatever it is you're currently doing.

I know that I talk a lot about success, because that's what we want, isn't it? Whether it's financial success, marital success, fitness success, or job success, it's out there for everyone if you just go out and get it.

Why not you?

Let's go back to recognizing the opportunity in front of you - just like the eagle does.

The eagle soars high above within the sky, he has sharp eyes, he has the ability to look down, he sees the food, the meal, the feast and he swoops down with great speed, he dives into the water he grabs his feast, he takes it with him and all because he recognizes his opportunity. He's not sitting in the nest having a pity party because things didn't go his way that day. The weather may be bad and his feathers may be ruffled, but he has to make things happen.

It is called Survival and Doing well.

We have to become more like the eagle and not the parrot. The parrot sits in his cage: "Feed me! Feed me!" Please take care of me. All he can do is to say, "Feed me," and maybe he'll say a few words. Don't be like the parrot, be like the eagle. This country was founded with this spirit, and it's the symbol of this great nation; be part of it, will you? After all, how many of you want more out of life, but don't know where to go and get it?

If I pointed you in the right direction and I gave you the right opportunity, how many of you would lose it though lack of effort or hard work? When I'm talking to sales managers and business owners and their employees, I often ask them this question,

"Would you go to work for you?" In other words, are you your best friend, or your worst enemy, what is your mind constantly telling you on a daily basis, what are you filling your mind with? What are you filling your body with? I hope good things. After reading my book you're going to practice what is in the book; positive attitude, spotting the opportunity and working hard to obtain it, that is all that is required for success. Promise me. Say "yes."

For those of you that want more, are you willing to pay the price, put up with the pain, and do whatever needs to be done to succeed? Colonel Sanders the founder of KFC, he literally knocked on a thousand doors before someone said, 'Yes, I'll buy your chicken recipe." How many of you would have quit, possibly after the one hundredth door.

You never know what you're made of, until you actually push yourself, that's why I ask managers and leaders in the community; "Would you go to work for yourself?" If the answer is "yes," then you're in the right position. If the answer is "no," chances are you can't lead people and you're in the wrong position, and your employees are not going to be effective and your family will be hurt as well.

How many times have you said to yourself, "If only I had done what I needed to do, when I needed to do it, I'd be much better off today." We all have, because regrets in life are something that we all run across on a day-to-day basis. What I'm trying to do and why I am excited and so intense about this, and why I spend so much time on the road and write my books, is to get people to recognize the opportunity in front of them; to have them "wake up" "get motivated," and have them "go after it," because if you don't, somebody else will. The government will not take care of you in the style that you truly desire.

I would like to caution you to be careful that you do not surround yourself with people who give you, what I call, "false hope;" those who give you delusions about who you really are, because a true critique of your life is critical to your success. Sometimes we're too hard or too soft on ourselves. How many people who are truly attractive think they're attractive; very few people do. How many of us are self-conscious about a certain thing about our body, yet people are constantly saying, "Hey, you're crazy!" Or, how about the woman whose 110 lbs. and thinks that she's overweight, and her friends are telling her, "You are not overweight you're okay," but still that nagging little person inside her mind is saying, "you're overweight, you're ugly, You're not up to speed, you can't do it."

Get counseling and feedback from somebody whom you respect and trust; someone that will help you to recognize opportunity, and help you develop your own personal talent. We have the tendency to get advice from people who are more messed up than we are.

If you cannot find a mentor then read my book "*Grow Your Company Grow Yourself: Together Dominate the Marketplace.*" *- Randy E. King 2010*

You will discover how to find where your best opportunity is, and how to grow once you have found it.

—*"For as he thinketh in his heart, so he is."*
Proverbs 23:7

Chapter 9

Inspiration & Thoughts:

Men, women and children speak about what it is to be an American

We created the American Pride blog to compliment storiesofusa.com. When you visit the site you have the ability to tell us your story. There are some heart-felt stories which will bring tears to your eyes; we did not adjust nor edit any of the stories.

Some names have been changed to protect the story tellers. There is one exception: Mr. Jan Weiss, it is his story and his post and I truly enjoyed giving him full credit for both.

"America, once an experiment unique in the world, is now the last best hope for the world. By making sacrifices for America, we bind ourselves to those great patriots who fought at Yorktown, Gettysburg, and Iwo Jima and prove ourselves worthy of the blessings of freedom. History will view America as a great gift to the world, a gift that Americans today must preserve and cherish." - *Heritage Foundation, Leadership for America*

Jim says:

"I was thinking about this site some more and this site was founded on the principle that Democrats, Republicans, all denominations of religion as long as you believe in God and our country could benefit and could have AMERICAN

PRIDE looking at this site. No other site on the internet lifts up God and Country, American Heroes and gives people a place to tell their patriotic stories...You and Mike have given people a place to build up hope again for America."

Marie says:

"THANK YOU for this special AMERICAN PRIDE web site. THANK YOU for reminding us what this great country stands for and for what you are doing for our children. Thank you for providing a forum to learn about American patriotism and a place for Americans to share their stories. THANK YOU to all who contribute to this site. THANK YOU to the children of Freedom Academy and a Special THANK YOU TO RANDY AND MIKE FOR THE LOVE AND DEVOTION IT TAKES TO PUT TOGETHER THIS BEAUTIFUL AMAZING WEB SITE, AND THANK YOU DOUG FOR WRITING AND SINGING."

"GLAD TO BE LIVIN IN THE USA." GOD BLESS YOU

Lillian says:

"We are so blessed to live in such a great country. May God richly bless and keep our service men and women safe. I have four brothers that served in the armed forces. One of them was in the Navy, one was in the Air Force and the other two served in the Army. My husband has two brothers that have served in the armed forces. One of them was in the Army and the other was in the Air Force. At the present time I have a grandson in the Navy. I have not seen him in his Navy uniform yet but you can bet when I do this will be one proud grandmother. I am so thankful for the time and sacrifice men and women have given for our freedom. May God continue to bless this great country and keep us free. I want to say thank you to each and every service man and woman in uniform. The men and women in the armed forces are the backbone of this country. Thank God for this great country. I am so proud of America."

Shelly says:

"How wonderful, especially to give them an accurate portrayal of American history; I am not familiar with the curriculum being taught, however, I imagine that it will not be skewed if we intend for our children to learn something. In addition, it is so important to begin raising awareness of our environment and how we can preserve it."

Lindsey says:

"If we don't appreciate what we have we will lose it. America needs to realize that Freedom can be taken away and well as given. Thank you for this site that reminds all of us that we should pay attention."

James says:

Thank you;

"IT IS OUR CONSTITUTION; DO YOU WANT TO KEEP IT OR WHAT? I SAY KEEP IT; ENFORCE IT; LIVE BY IT! There comes a time when the people of a nation must take charge of their government and answer for it. Since I never believed in the word impossible I now stand before you telling you we can and will bring our gove…rnment back to its founding roots, THIS I WILL DO!!! If I do nothing else!

There is so much more we can do but only together. Do not give up! We do have a future; yes I'm a presidential candidate for 2012. We must understand, that Society is a blessing, but government, even at its best state, is a necessary evil; in its worst state an intolerable one; when we exposed to the same miseries which we might expect in a country without government! Our ability to control and change our future is the ability to unite together. For together we can."

Quinton says:

"I am 25 years old. The problem I have noticed with some of the generation before me, the majority of my generation, and all of the generations behind me is it has become cool to be Un-American and Unpatriotic. You are made fun of, laughed at, teased, and thought of as "weird" if you like and support our country.

This problem has been brought on by ignorant people and parents who have not taken the time to educate their children on how privileged we are in America. Kids brought up now a day's have no idea what it is like in other countries. They have no idea how restricted life is outside of our borders. Because of this, they cannot begin to comprehend the freedoms we are given. Freedoms we are just given, we don't have to work for them, they are freely given to us on a daily basis because generations before us fought and died for them.

Are generations are being brought up and let to do whatever they want, whenever they want, and they have nobody to discipline them, no one to set them straight, and no reper-cussion for their miss-conducted actions. Parents have become afraid to discipline their children. Heaven forbid they get caught spanking their child; authorities may be called on them for such a thing. Our future generations are being brought up with no respect, no manners, and no knowledge of our country and its history. Our countries' history classes are being stripped from our schools are replaced with foreign country histories. I believe educating our generations on other countries is a wonderful idea, but it needs to be used to solidify our country and used for examples of how privileged we are. Not to damage and poison our own country.

With the way things are going I see, in the not to distance future, generations that will once again be forced to fight and die for freedoms we once had because we did not properly educate and discipline our future generations in order to secure our future freedoms."

Professor Orlando says:

"For most of human history, and for nearly all of the non-Western world prior to Western contact, freedom was, and for many still remains, anything but an obvious or desirable goal. Other values and ideals were, or are, of far greater importance to them-values such as the pursuit of glory, honor, and power for oneself or one's family and clan, nationalism, and imperial grandeur, militarism and valor in warfare, filial piety, the harmony of heaven and earth, the spreading of the "true faith", nirvana, hedonism, altruism, justice, equality, material progress-the list is endless. But almost never, outside the context of Western culture and its influence, has it included freedom.

Indeed, non-Western peoples have thought so little about freedom that most human languages did not even possess a word for the concept before contact with the West."

Proud Marine says:

"Every time I jump on this site, I find Hope and inspiration that America will continue to be the greatest nation there is. Marines don't cry, their eyes sweat, and mine have done that many times looking at the American nuggets that are within this site. I just pulled up the Statue of Liberty and played to first video. What a touching song."

Wish I could see him again says:

"My father served in the military. I never knew him very well. Growing up as an only child, he worked all the time to support the family. As I grew up and as i today am his age when i look back, I wish that we spent more time together. He died at a very early age and did not get to enjoy his retirement! I wish that I could have one more conversation with my father! I have 2 young children and will not make the mistake of not getting to know them. When they push me away with their busy schedules and it's not cool to kiss or hug them in front of their friends, well, that's just too bad. I wish that my father would have hugged me more. This site brings me and my boys together…thank you."

Patriot Mom says:

"You will never know how much it has cost my generation to preserve your freedom. I hope you will make good use of it. JOHN QUINCY ADAMS. How little do my countrymen know what precious blessings they are in possession of and which no other people on earth enjoy. THOMAS JEFFERSON. We need an America with the wisdom of experience, but we must never let America grow old in spirit. A good leader can't get too far ahead of his followers. FRANKLIN ROOSEVELT. IT IS IMPOSSIBLE TO RIGHTLY GOVERN THE WORLD WITHOUT GOD AND THE BIBLE. I believe with all my heart that one cannot be American President with a belief in God without the strength that faith gives you. GEORGE H.W.BUSH THE BIBLE WAS IMPORTANT TO MANY AMERICAN PRESIDENTS."

GOD BLESS THE USA.

LOVING YOUR COUNTRY – Jan Weiss

"Look at your baby, and you will see a new individual, with its own proteins, its own DNA, and its own eyes. It has its own soul and will build its own mind. Each one of your babies will be different and will be different from all others,

This has been happening in every family for thousands of years. It has created many different races and many different nations. And we always have seen the same problem. What shall be the relationship between people and races and nations?

History has taught us this relationship is either exclusively one of self- love, or of love to the other person. Self -love leads to theft, violence and murder. Love to the neighbor inspires service to others outside of oneself.

To groups individuals will express love to the neighbor as

love for a church, a society or a country, or even to all countries. But in this talk we will only deal with the love of one's country.

For centuries people have organized themselves into countries that have lived either in peace or in a state of war. We should never attack another country, but if we are attacked by another country, we are allowed to defend our own country from the love we have for our own country.

Loving our own country excludes the desire to attack another country, and attacking another country really excludes loving our own country. just as attacking another person excludes loving another person.

Life is really very simple: We either choose to love ourselves or we choose to love others, we are either in hell or in heaven, and this will be the same in the material world or the spiritual world, and after death".

WORLD WAR 2 EXPERIENCES – Jan Weiss

PERIODS OF WW2

There were several periods in the war:

1. Before WW2
2. Entering WW2
3. During WW2
4. Exiting WW2
5. After WW2

BEFORE WW2

1. I was born in Holland in 1927, and I spent the first part of my life in the Netherlands. World War 2 started in 1940

when I was 13, and finished in 1945 when I was 18.

2. Warning Against Hitler

Hitler wrote a book, Mein Kampf (My fight), and in that book he wrote what thought and what he was going to do. I can remember one of my high school teachers who had this book on his desk, and was reading it even while he was teaching us. In that book Hitler wrote how he wanted to conquer other countries. How he was going to treat the Jews in every nation he occupied. He did this in several stages.

First he would distinguish them from the others (Arians) by insisting they wear the Jewish star on all their clothing. Then they were systematically arrested, and transported to concentration camps in Germany. In those concentration camps they were systematically gassed and cremated. So Hitler himself warned us against himself and his ideas.

3. Oldest Brother's Prophecy

I can remember my oldest brother (5 years older) talking at the evening table, and warning us against Hitler. The others at the table criticized him for this talk, and disliked him for it. But he could not stop talking. My parents and the other brothers did not read daily papers, and so they were kind of ignorant in comparison.

4. Some Followed Warning.

I remember an author who sailed across the North Sea to England before the war started. I remember an American minister who traveled from Holland through Belgium, France, into Spain, and sailed from there to America. But most of us were caught by the Germans in Holland and experienced 5 years of Nazi occupation.

5. Warning by Dutch Spy

I remember hearing about a Dutch spy who operated in Germany and warned the Dutch government that the Germans were planning an invasion into Holland. But the government did not listen, and on the first day of invasion German soldiers came out of a ship that had been parked in the harbor of Rotterdam.

6. Mobilization summer 1939

My family used to spend each summer a whole month in Katwijk at the sea, where we spent every day at the sea. My father used to rent a car that would bring the whole family from Rotterdam to Katwijk, with all our belonging. He would rent a whole house, where we would have an evening meal and where we would sleep. In the day we would spend the whole day on the sand and in the water, and my father would sit in a chair and talk to various people about education.

But in the summer of 1939 the Dutch government mobilized the country, and so we could not use the car to return to Rotterdam, and so my father rented with another family a bus, and we returned to Rotterdam in that bus. This was the beginning of a whole change of our life.

ENTERING WW2

On May 5th German planes dropped soldiers from the air into Rotterdam. They also crossed the border between Germany and Holland. Then they also bombed the center of Rotterdam, so much of it burnt down. We saw people streaming out of the center, seeking new housing in outskirt areas. We saw many houses burnt down.

In the meantime German soldiers marched to the Hague where we had the center of the Dutch government, and on May 10th Holland capitulated, and Nazi government began, and would reign for 5 years. It was an easy take. Any resistance was crushed down with force and speed.

DURING WW2

1. Not much change

In the beginning we did not notice much change. German soldiers were very disciplined. One time a soldier took something from a young boy on a street car. He went to the German commandant, who took him around his soldiers to identify the thief, and when the soldier was identified and he confessed, he was shot and killed by the commandant on the spot.

But slowly circumstances began to change. Less and less food in the stores, and also less and less supplies. In the last year of the war all stores were empty and closed. Also there was no electricity, gas, or coal, only water.

2. Price of Food

My father bought a loaf of bread on the black market, and paid for it a laborer's monthly salary, and then we would stay in bed much of the day, and have one slice of bread per day, and that was all the food we had.

3. Sugar Beets

One day in the winter of 1944 my brother and I pushed a wheel cart for half a day to get a heap of sugar beets out of a field to bring it home for our family. On the way back I was so hungry that I took a sugar beet, bit into the clay and spit it out until I reached the meat of the beet.

4. Heating and Light

Our hearth was removed, and we bought a little hearth where we could burn wood or coal. The wood was cut from the trees in parks or from bomb shelters. The coal was dug out of the paths in parks. On that little hearth my mother cooked if she had food. It heated the room where it was installed, and at night we sat around the little hearth where we could see just a little. I remember we created electricity with the dynamo on a bicycle, so some of us could read.

5. Underground Experiences

In the last year of the war I was in the underground. We gathered in school gymnasiums where we practiced with brenguns and stenguns. I was able to put a these weapons together blindfolded. But first I had to meet every person at their house and then bring him to the gymnasium whose location they did not know.

6. Gathering News

When the invasion started it became important to gather invasion news, which was not available on the Dutch radio, but only on the English radio. My father did not allow us to this, so one of my friends did it, and typed out the news every day, which I then followed on the map, seeing the allied forces advance from LeHavre all the way into Europe.

One day I approached my friend's house to get the news, and I saw the German police from a distance, and so I quickly turned back on my path. Later I learned that most of the people who worked on the news had escaped over the roof, but the parents of my friend were arrested, and later on executed.

7. Work Forces

The Germans often arrested males and made them work in Germany. They would barricade a street, and then go from door to door, and get the men out of the house. My mother was smart. She told the soldier that we were sick in bed with an infectious disease. The soldier refused to go near us.

8. Accidental Arrest

My oldest brother was hiding from the Germans, and staying with a family. The German police were after a certain person. They knew his name and the name of the person where he was staying. When they came into the village they asked children for the name of his host, the children pointed to the house of another person with the same name, and that was the host of my oldest brother. So my brother was arrested, first brought to a Dutch concentration camp, and from there to a German concentration camp. After arrival, one of the guards looked at his records, and noticed my brother was "polizilich unbekannt" (not known with the police), and so they let him out of the concentration camp, but made him work in a police station.

9. Bombing by Allied Forces

To prepare the Germans for the invasion, night after night allied planes would fly from England deep into Germany, where they would bomb and destroy many cities. At first we would flee into the cellar, but after a while we would stay in bed and sleep through these operations.

10. Razzia at College

At the end of the war it was dangerous to go to college. One time we had to run from the back of the building, because German soldiers were trying to get into the front of the building, so they could reach students to get them to work for them.

I safely got to the rail road station and rode on the train to Rotterdam, but we then decided that we could not go to college anymore. After the war I returned to the college, but for quite a while I had to ride the train standing in a cattle car, because the Germans had taken all our passenger train cars, and we had to search for them all over Germany.

EXITING WW2

1. Final Day

When we found out that the Germans had lost the war and had given up, we were all very excited, and after curfew time, when we were not allowed to be on the street (6pm), we went outside and began to share that information and joy.

At a certain moment a convertible with 3 German soldiers drove into our street, stood up in the car, and shouted "Hinein" (Go inside). At that moment it was clear how scared we still were of the Germans, for people ran to their doors and tried to get in, but some doors were closed, and people could not get in.

2. Whole Night of Dancing from street to street

Once we were sure the German occupation had come to an

end, we went from street to street for a whole night, singing and dancing for joy. The five years of German occupation had been very hard and scared us a lot.

AFTER WW2

1. Back to College

After WW2 it was safe to go back to college, and I could sit in the train again.

2. Return of Oldest Brother

One day after the war, our whole family was together in our parental home. And suddenly we heard a key slide into the outdoor lock, the door was opened, and we heard someone come into the house. We were startled, for every key holder was already inside. Who could this be? We spontaneously all ran to the door! And here was my oldest brother. He had walked all the way from Oranienburg, Germany to our home. How excited we all were. We did not know he was still alive, as we thought he was in a concentration camp until the end of the war.

But do not think he told us much. He talked a little, but then asked where his girlfriend lived, and then on a borrowed bicycle he drove to her to tell about his return. And even after he returned to the parental home, he told us very little about his concentration camp experiences.

All he told us was the fact that at one time he had been discharged from the concentration camp because he was told he was "polizeilich nicht bekannt" (=not know by the police, they did not know why he was there). Then they made him work on the furnace of a police station, where had enough food and was always warm.

3. Threat of Communistic Russia

By the time I had graduated from the chemical engineering college, we became aware of another threat, namely from communistic Russia. And I was glad to be able to go to the United States in 1950. When I arrived on the boat in the New York harbor and saw the statue of liberty, I felt happy and safe! No more dictators in my life, please!

4. Thanks to the Allied Forces

I will never forget how many men in the Allied Forces died for my liberation from Hitler and his Nazis. It is now 65 years ago that the Second World War ended, and my memories are still very vivid. Sometimes I hear people talk about casualties in more recent wars, but none of them can compare in any way with the casualties of World War 2. So thanks to all those young men who probably have forgotten this war. Even today I hope to do something for their children, grandchildren and great grandchildren.

Keeping the American Spirit alive
and well for generations to follow

Thanks to all that wrote to us, and go online
at www.storiesofusa.com and read more stories.

Chapter 10

The World Came to See America

"There's the country of America, which you have to defend, but there's also the idea of America. America is more than just a country, it's an idea. An idea that's supposed to be contagious."
—Bono

I am so fired up! At the time of writing this book over 146 countries have visited the web-site www.storiesofusa.com- amazing. And they came within 120 days of when it was launched and more countries are coming everyday.

There are 195 countries in the world today.

Unless you don't count Taiwan…

Taiwan is not considered an official country by many, which would bring the count down to 194 countries. Although Taiwan operates as an independent country, many countries (including the U.S.) do not officially recognize it as one. Because the People's Republic of China considers Taiwan a breakaway province of China, countries who wish to maintain diplomatic relations with China have had to sever their formal relations with Taiwan (more than 100 countries, however, have unofficial relations with Taiwan).

How many countries belong to the United Nations?

192 countries are UN members. The exceptions are Taiwan (in 1971, the UN ousted Taiwan and replaced it with the People's Republic of China) and Vatican City. Kosovo is not yet a member. The newest UN members are Switzerland (2002) and Montenegro (2006).

What are the world's newest countries?

The world's newest country is Kosovo, which declared independence from Serbia in February 2008. Before that, the newest country was Montenegro, which became a country in June 2006, after splitting off from Serbia. Since 1990, 28 new nations have come into being. Many of these emerged from the collapse of the Soviet Union (14 countries) and the breakup of the former Yugoslavia (7 countries). See our Guide to New Nations.

Are there still any countries that have colonies?

There are 61 colonies or territories in the world. Eight countries maintain them: Australia (6), Denmark (2), Netherlands (2), France (16), New Zealand (3), Norway (3), the United Kingdom (15), and the United States (14). Are there still territories in the world that are claimed by more than one country?

There are six major disputed territories in the world: The Paracel Islands, Spratly Islands, Western Sahara, and Antarctica (about a dozen nations have laid claims to portions of it). In addition, there are innumerable other territorial disputes throughout the world, many of which had resulted in ongoing armed conflicts.[8]

How the Website Started for the World to Show Up!

I had an essay contest for the entire student body, grades one through eight, at the Freedom Academy in Scottsdale, Arizona. The 3 questions asked were:

1. What America means to me.
2. What would do you want the future of America to look like.
3. What do you feel the future of America will look like?

My staff and I picked a winner from each grade for the essay contest. Another student compiled the sound track and pictures to create the America Pride eBook.

When the eBook was completed, I wanted to find an effective way to distribute it to the active American service men and women. I just happened to show up at 8:00am at a print shop in La Habra, CA, by the name of University Printing, waiting for the same printer was a person who designed and marketed websites by the name of Mike Beaumont. I had previously met Mike about a year ago, and began our conversation. In that conversation, we discussed some aspects of the project; it lasted for about 45 minutes. Another meeting was scheduled in the afternoon at a local restaurant. After another hour long conversation, Mike had a clear understanding of the goals that I had and Mike formulated a plan on how to achieve them. At that point, we began to put our plan into action. After two solid weeks of research, web-site coding and in addition a large amount of content, StoriesofUSA. com was created. We wanted to do more than just create a marketing piece for an eBook. We wanted to develop both a multimedia resource of American history and an interactive forum for Americans to tell their patriotic stories.

When we developed Storiesofusa.com, we never dreamed that over 146 countries within 3 months would visit the site and see what America was all about. We wanted Stories of USA to be their personal study guide of *American Patriotism* and also *How to Be a Success in America.*

We guarantee that if you spend the time studying and understanding the easy to follow information in this site, you will gain the knowledge and skills necessary to be a successful American and understand that your success was brought to you in part by living and working hard in the United States of America.

People from other nations came and stayed to view our history. They received lessons on:

Understanding the Past

- Famous People in United States History
- Famous Locations in United States History
- Important American Documents & Speeches
- Important Events in United States History that Shaped America

Appreciating the Present

- Important National Icons
- Patriotic Holidays & Activities

Preparing for the Future

- Learning Skills to Become Successful Adults
- Participation in Personal **Development** Activities

Our Vision

American patriotism is alive a well today in the United States of America. I believe that the United States of America is truly a great country; not because of our ability to win wars; not because of our abundant natural resources; but because we share a common culture of laws, charity, freedom, liberty, hard work, dedication to family & spirituality and the willingness to sacrifice oneself for the betterment of the Nation as a whole.

It is imperative that we pass these uniquely American values to the next generation, because "Soon It Will Be Their Choice."

United States History is more than just a series of events and historical characters. It is a living and breathing entity which affects our Nation and our culture. One person can and does make a difference for the positive and for the negative. Through video, pictures, text and interaction, we describe how we are a product of history and that the United States of America, its culture and American Patriotism have been forged through a number of significant events that have created who we are today.

StoriesofUSA.com was developed to work along with American Pride eBook, and was designed primarily for the following four reasons:

1. Provide a brief history to help explain the most important historical events in the making of the United States of America.
2. Express the guiding principles and documents of the United States of America.
3. Describe the Nation's major Historical Icons.
4. Provide a forum for America's youth to learn about

American patriotism and for all Americans (especially youth and veterans) to share their stories of *What it Means to Be an American.*

Our Primary Goals:

1. Provide a place for young Americans to learn about the United States of America and to share their patriotic stories about America.
2. Distribute AmericanPrideeBook.com and StoriesofUSA.com to our active military and veterans.

How You Can Help Us:

The American Pride eBook is a FREE eBook that contains both an audio soundtrack and a visual pictorial display. The eBook was developed by children for children.

1. Sit back and watch the American Pride eBook
2. Share this eBook with others through as many ways as you can think of, including: Facebook, email and Twitter.
3. Put your name and email address in the form on the right side of this website. Also, become a fan of our Facebook fan page. There is a Facebook link on the right side of this web-site. This will help us make it easy to provide you with current news and information.

Our Philosophy:

AmericanPrideeBook.com and StoriesofUSA.com are not for or against any political party, race, gender or religion. Its purpose is to provide a brief history of America's past and a forum for patriotic Americans to share their stories of what it means to be an American.

We encourage you to participate in viewing the eBook and telling your story. Please refrain from vulgar language.

History is more than just a series of events and historical characters. It is a living and breathing entity which affects everyone. Past events affect future events. One person can and does make a difference for the positive and for the negative.

"The great American legacy of FREEDOM and DEMOCRACY
will soon be in the hands of our children"
– Randy E. King

Our Mission:

1. Provide a place for young Americans to learn about American Patriotism and to share their patriotic stories about America.
2. Distribute AmericanPrideeBook.com and StoriesofUSA. com to our youth, active military, veterans and those interested in learning about American Patriotism.
3. Educate our youth on how to become successful Americans.

Why Multiple Languages:

We do believe than a strong understanding of the English language is important to becoming a success in the United States of America. We also believe that it should not be a barrier to appreciating the values and culture that makes America great. If individuals truly want to become part of American society, they will do what it takes to communicate effectively. English, Spanish and French are languages spoken and understood by a significant percentage of the world's population. That is why these languages have been chosen.

Chapter 11

My Green Tree Theory of Leadership in America

No, this is not an Environmental story.
It's a story about dumb leaders vs. smart leaders...

"The fool wonders, the wise man asks."
—Benjamin Disraeli

Two Blind mice and one who can see: a parable I have what I call a Green Tree Theory of America First blind mouse.

Suppose you have three Leaders in the country, all with the task of building a stronger America. You tell them night is falling and they have to build a fire to stay warm and to keep the people warm.

The unsuccessful Leader sits there and looks at all those trees in front of him. What does he do? He ignores the old trees that would make great firewood and he chops down the green trees!

Why did he choose the green trees?

He chose the green trees because that's all he sees. Is the mouse color-Blind?

Our unsuccessful Leader of our Country can't differentiate between good firewood and the green trees. They all look the same to him.

He chops down green trees and puts them on the fire, thinking to himself, "I'm going to really get a blazing fire."

With all the good intentions in the world, fully expecting success, he goes through a whole book or two of matches and can't figure out why his fire isn't starting.

He thinks it must be the matches. He can't be wrong, so it's the matches fault. It can't be anything he's doing.

Do you see the problem?

Take the blindfolds off your mind.

Our unsuccessful Leader spends days reinventing a new match. He makes the match hotter. He knows it's going to have a huge spark, and knows it's going to really fire up his group of green trees. In the meantime while he was making the matches (and freezing in the cold nights) it rained on his green trees. Now it's even more difficult to create the fire he needs.

Our unsuccessful Leader tries again. Surely, his bigger match will light the fire!

Nothing happens, of course.

YOU can never win in the blame game.

He takes another look at his pile of green trees in the fire pit—and, zap!—he decides it must be bad trees. (!!!) He'll always blame something or someone else, never himself, for his failures: The previous administration will do.

He goes back into the forest and he cuts down a fresh batch of green trees. He repeats the above over and over, always wondering why other leaders are more successful, but never asking anyone, especially successful leaders, for their help.

The Second Blind Mouse.

The second style of governing; the leader looks at the forest and cuts down the whole forest and puts it all in the fire pit. There's enough dry wood in the forest that he'll get a fire, but achieving the result is much more difficult. At least the outcome will be better—there is a fire—but it requires a huge amount of effort.

This leader plugs along and just flat out makes it happen— but with twice as much work as necessary.

The Born Leader.

The third style of leadership in my Green Tree Theory of America is the type of Leader who has an innate ability to recognize the good firewood instantly. This Leader does not confuse the green trees with the old trees; this Leader knows that older trees make the best firewood and that green trees will not burn no matter what he does. Once in a while this Leader chops a little green tree with the other good firewood trees, but notices right away that the green tree makes smoke but no fire, and doesn't do it again.

Learn from your mistakes.

What One Can DO—ALL You Can DO.

Some politicians will read this book and apply my principles and still will not get the country where it needs to be.

Our Leaders Must Learn by Their Mistakes.

I know our Leaders will sit there and keep those same green trees in the fire pit and keep using the same matches. They'll light and light, to the point that one day they wake up and say, "Uh-oh, I don't have the strength to light anymore."

Winter sets in, and the country freezes to death.

In other words, that Leader needs to know when they are taking the country in the wrong direction and change course.

Some of our Politicians have big egos. They don't know when to be able to humble themselves and ask for help when they need it. They don't just surround themselves with people who agree with them and stroke their ego.

Successful Leaders are interesting, because the more successful they are the more they want to help others to achieve success. They want everyone in our great Country to achieve success and not take from the successful and give to the lazy. The successful Leader wants to show you how to become successful not take away from the successful.

Chapter 12

Meanings - Terminology and Definitions

"Truth is violated by falsehood; it may be equally outraged by not fully understanding and getting faked out."
—Randy E King

Over the years I have seen and heard a lot of terms thrown around very lightly, frankly, many people using the terms were, let's just say, not well informed. So when I decided to write this book, I wanted to include a chapter on some of the most commonly used terminology, that both sides of the political spectrum have used over the years. What follows should bring thought and clarity to some of those frequently used terms.

United States of America

— *noun*

(*functioning as singular or plural*) **United States, US,** Often shortened to: **USA** a federal republic mainly in North America consisting of 50 states and the District of Columbia: colonized principally by the English and French in the 17th century, the native Indians being gradually defeated and displaced; 13 colonies under British rule made the Declaration of Independence in 1776 and became the United States after the War of American Independence. The northern states defeated the South in the Civil War (1861-65). It is the world's most productive industrial nation and also exports agricultural products. It consists generally of the Rocky Mountains in the west, the Great Plains in the center, the Appalachians in the east, deserts in the southwest and coastal lowlands and swamps in the southeast. Language: predominantly English; Spanish is also widely spoken. Religion: Christian majority. Currency: dollar. Capital: Washington, DC. Pop: 297 043 000 (2004 est). Area: 9 518 323 sq km (3 675 031 sq miles)

con·sti·tu·tion

noun \ kän(t)-stə-ˈtü-shən, -ˈtyü-\

Definition of *CONSTITUTION*

1: an established law or custom : ORDINANCE

2 *a* : the physical makeup of the individual especially with respect to the health, strength, and appearance of the body <a hearty *constitution*> *b* : the structure, composition, physical makeup, or nature of something <the *constitution* of society>

3: the act of establishing, making, or setting up

4: the mode in which a state or society is organized; *especially* : the manner in which sovereign power is distributed

5 *a* : the basic principles and laws of a nation, state, or social group that determine the powers and duties of the government and guarantee certain rights to the people in it *b* : a written instrument embodying the rules of a political or social organization

Definition of *DICTATORSHIP*

dic•ta•tor•ship

noun \dik-ˈtā-tər-ˌship, ˈdik-ˌ

1: the office of DICTATOR

2: autocratic rule, control, or leadership

3 *a*: a form of government in which absolute power is concentrated in a DICTATOR or a small clique *b*: a government organization or group in which absolute power is so concentrated *c*: a despotic state

de·moc·ra·cy

Pronunciation: di-'mä-kr&-sE Function: *noun*

Inflected Form: *plural* **-cies**

1 a : government by the people; *especially* : rule of the majority **b :** a government in which the supreme power is vested in the people and exercised by them directly or indirectly through a system of representation usually involving periodically held free elections **2 :** a political unit that has a democratic government — **dem·o·crat·ic** /"de-m&-'kra-tik/ *adjective* — **dem·o·crat·i·cal·ly** *adverb*

cap·i·tal·ism

Spelled [**kap**-i-tl-iz-*uh*m]

—noun

an economic system in which investment in and ownership of the means of production, distribution, and exchange of wealth is made and maintained chiefly by private individuals or corporations, esp. as contrasted to cooperatively or state-owned means of wealth.

Dictionary.com

Origin:

1850–55; capital¹+ -ism

—Related forms

an·ti·cap·i·tal·ism, *noun*

pro·cap·i·tal·ism, *noun*

free enterprise

—noun

1. An economic and political doctrine holding that a capitalist economy can regulate itself in a freely competitive market through the relationship of supply and demand with a minimum of governmental intervention and regulation.

2. The practice of free enterprise in an economy, or the right to practice it.

Also called **private enterprise.**

—Related forms

free-en·ter·pris·ing, *adjective*

so·cial·ism

Spelled [**soh**-sh*uh*-liz-*uh*m]

—noun

1. A theory or system of social organization that advocates the vesting of the ownership and control of the means of production and distribution, of capital, land, etc., in the community as a whole.

2. Procedure or practice in accordance with this theory.

3. (In Marxist theory) the stage following capitalism in the transition of a society to communism, characterized by the imperfect implementation of collectivist principles.

Compare <u>utopian socialism</u>.

sem·i·so·cial·ism, *noun*

un·so·cial·ism, *noun*

com·mu·nism

Spelled [**kom**-y*uh*-niz-*uh*m]

—*noun*

1. A theory or system of social organization based on the holding of all property in common, actual ownership being ascribed to the community as a whole or to the state.

2. (often *initial capital letter*) a system of social organization in which all economic and social activity is controlled by a totalitarian state dominated by a single and self-perpetuating political party.

3. (Initial *capital letter*) the principles and practices of the Communist party.

—*Related forms*

an·ti·com·mu·nism, *noun*

pro·com·mun·ism, *noun, adjective*

in·de·pend·ence

Spelled [in-di-**pen**-d*uh*ns]

—*noun*

1. Also, **<u>independency.</u>** The state or quality of being independent.

2. Freedom from the control, influence, support, aid, or the like, of others.

3. *Archaic.* a <u>competency</u>.

pol·i·tics

Spelled [**pol**-i-tiks]

–noun (*used with a singular or plural verb*)

1. The science or art of political government.

2. The practice or profession of conducting political affairs.

3. Political affairs: *The advocated reforms have become embroiled in politics.*

4. Political methods or maneuvers: *We could not approve of his politics in winning passage of the bill.*

5. Political principles or opinions: *We avoided discussion of religion and politics. His politics are his own affair.*

6. Use of intrigue or strategy in obtaining any position of power or control, as in business, university, etc.

7. (*initial capital letter, italics*) a treatise (4th century b.c.) by Aristotle, dealing with the structure, organization, and administration of the state, esp. the city-state as known in ancient Greece.

—Idiom

8. play politics,

a. to engage in political intrigue, take advantage of a political situation or issue, resort to partisan politics, etc.; exploit a political system or political relationships.

b. to deal with people in an opportunistic, manipulative, or devious way, as for job advancement.

—Related forms

an·ti·pol·i·tics, *adjective*

pro·pol·i·tics, *adjective*

in·di·vid·u·al·ism

Spelled[in-d*uh*-**vij**-oo-*uh*-liz-*uh*m]

—noun

1. a social theory advocating the liberty, rights, or independent action of the individual.

2. the principle or habit of or belief in independent thought or action.

3. the pursuit of individual rather than common or collective interests; egoism.

4. individual character; individuality.

5. an individual peculiarity.

6. *Philosophy.*

a. the doctrine that only individual things are real.

b. the doctrine or belief that all actions are determined by, or at least take place for, the benefit of the individual, not of society as a whole.

—Related forms

o·ver·in·di·vid·u·al·ism, *noun*

su·per·in·di·vid·u·al·ism, *noun*

tyr·an·ny

Spelled[**tir**-*uh*-nee]

—noun, plural -nies.

1. arbitrary or unrestrained exercise of power; despotic abuse of authority.

2. the government or rule of a tyrant or absolute ruler.

3. a state ruled by a tyrant or absolute ruler.

4. oppressive or unjustly severe government on the part of any ruler.

5. undue severity or harshness.

—Related forms

pre·tyr·an·ny, *noun, plural* -nies.

—Synonyms

1. despotism, absolutism, dictatorship.

Next time someone uses one of these terms, or better yet you have the desire to fire off a few of these, you will be well equipped with the meanings of the words you are using.[9]

Chapter 13

Great Quotes About Our Great Nation

Note: Not all these authors are from the U.S.A.; however, the sentiments can be applied to patriotism all around the globe.[10]

"I like to see a man proud of the place in which he lives. I like to see a man live so that his place will be proud of him"
~Abraham Lincoln

"America is a tune. It must be sung together"
~Gerald Stanley Lee, Crowds

"We can't all be Washington's, but we can all be patriots"
~Charles F. Browne

"What is the essence of America? Finding and maintaining that perfect, delicate balance between freedom "to" and freedom "from"
~Marilyn vos Savant, in Parade

"[P]atriotism... is not short, frenzied outbursts of emotion, but the tranquil and steady dedication of a lifetime"
~Adlai Stevenson

*"A man's country is not a certain area of land,
of mountains, rivers, and woods, but it is a principle;
and patriotism is loyalty to that principle"*
~George William Curtis

*"When an American says that he loves his country,
he means not only that he loves the New England hills,
the prairies glistening in the sun, the wide and rising plains,
the great mountains, and the sea. He means that he loves an inner
air, an inner light in which freedom lives and in which a man can
draw the breath of self-respect"*
~Adlai Stevenson

*"Love your country. Your country is the land where your parents
sleep, where is spoken that language in which the chosen of your
heart, blushing, whispered the first word of love;
it is the home that God has given you that by striving to perfect
yourselves therein you may prepare to ascend to him"*
~Giuseppe Mazzini

*"There are those, I know, who will say that the liberation of humanity, the freedom of man and mind, is nothing but a dream.
They are right. It is the American dream"*
~Archibald MacLeish

"National honor is national property of the highest value"
~James Monroe, first inaugural address, 4 March 1817

GREAT QUOTES ABOUT OUR GREAT NATION   243

"How often we fail to realize our good fortune in living in a country where happiness is more than a lack of tragedy"
~Paul Sweeney

"May the sun in his course visit no land more free, more happy, more lovely, than this our own country"
~Daniel Webster

"This nation will remain the land of the free only so long as it is the home of the brave"
~Elmer Davis

"The stern hand of fate has scourged us to an elevation where we can see the great everlasting things that matter for a nation; the great peaks of honor we had forgotten - duty and patriotism, clad in glittering white; the great pinnacle of sacrifice pointing like a rugged finger to heaven"
~David Lloyd George

"Yet America is a poem in our eyes; its ample geography dazzles the imagination, and it will not wait long for metres"
~Ralph Waldo Emerson, "*The Poet*," Essays, Second Series, 1844

"If our country is worth dying for in time of war let us resolve that it is truly worth living for in time of peace"
~Hamilton Fish

"And I'm proud to be an American, where at least I know I'm free. And I won't forget the men who died, who gave that right to me"
~Lee Greenwood

"The cement of this union is the heart-blood of every American"
~Thomas Jefferson

"America is much more than a geographical fact.
It is a political and moral fact - the first community in which men
set out in principle to institutionalize freedom,
responsible government, and human equality"
~Adlai Stevenson

"From every mountain side Let Freedom ring"
~Samuel F. Smith, "America"

"Ours is the only country deliberately founded on a good idea"
~John Gunther

"America is a passionate idea or it is nothing.
America is a human brotherhood or it is chaos"
~Max Lerner, *Actions and Passions*, 1949

"Then join hand in hand, brave Americans all!
By uniting we stand, by dividing we fall"
~John Dickinson

"The skies of happiness shine upon these United States of America"
~Terri Guillemets

"If you are ashamed to stand by your colors,
you had better seek another flag"
~Author Unknown

"Where liberty dwells, there is my country"
~Benjamin Franklin

"Liberty and Union, now and forever, one and inseparable"
~Daniel Webster

*"If you take advantage of everything America has to offer,
there's nothing you can't accomplish"*
~Geraldine Ferraro

*"Oh, it's home again and home again, America for me!
I want a ship that's westward bound to plough the rolling sea
To the blessed land of Room enough beyond the ocean bars,
Where the air is full of sunlight and the flag is full of stars"*
~Henry Van Dyke

*"Sometimes people call me an idealist.
Well, that is the way I know I am an American.
America is the only idealistic nation in the world"*
~Woodrow Wilson

*"This, then, is the state of the union: free and restless, growing
and full of hope. So it was in the beginning. So it shall always be,
while God is willing, and we are strong enough to keep the faith"*
~Lyndon B. Johnson

*"We sleep peacefully at night,
cradled by the big strong hands of America"*
~Val Saintsbury

"America is another name for opportunity.
Our whole history appears like a last effort of divine providence on
behalf of the human race"
~Ralph Waldo Emerson

"I love my freedom. I love my America"
~Jessi Lane Adams

"This country will not be a good place for any of us to live in unless
we make it a good place for all of us to live in"
~Theodore Roosevelt

"Of all the supervised conditions for life offered man,
those under USA's constitution have proved the best. Wherefore, be
sure when you start modifying, corrupting or abrogating it"
~Martin H. Fischer

"He loves his country best who strives to make it best"
~Robert G. Ingersoll

"It is the love of country that has lighted and that keeps
glowing the holy fire of patriotism"
~J. Horace McFarland

"Our country, right or wrong."
When right to be kept right; when wrong to be put right"
~Carl Schurz

"Off with your hat, as the flag goes by!
And let the heart have its say; you're man enough
for a tear in your eye that you will not wipe away"
~Henry Cuyler Bunner

"It is the flag just as much of the man who was naturalized yester-day as of the men whose people have been here many generations"
~Henry Cabot Lodge

*"The winds that blow through the wide sky in these mounts,
the winds that sweep from Canada to Mexico, from the Pacific
to the Atlantic - have always blown on free men"*
~Franklin D. Roosevelt

*"Some Americans need hyphens in their names,
because only part of them has come over;
but when the whole man has come over,
heart and thought and all,
the hyphen drops of its own weight out of his name"*
~Woodrow Wilson

*"My God! How little do my countrymen know what precious
blessings they are in possession of,
and which no other people on earth enjoy"*
~Thomas Jefferson

"America, for me, has been the pursuit and catching of happiness"
~Aurora Raigne

"I wish that every human life might be pure transparent freedom"
~Simone de Beauvoir

*"There is nothing wrong with America that
cannot be cured by what is right with America"*
~William J. Clinton

*"My favorite thing about the United States?
Lots of Americans, one America"*
~Val Saintsbury

*"Our country is not the only thing to which we owe our allegiance.
It is also owed to justice and to humanity. Patriotism consists not
in waving the flag, but in striving that our country
shall be righteous as well as strong"*
~James Bryce

*"Our great modern Republic. May those who seek the blessings
of its institutions and the protection of its flag remember
the obligations they impose"*
~Ulysses S. Grant

"For what avail the plough or sail, or land or life, if freedom fail"
~Ralph Waldo Emerson

*"Those who won our independence believed liberty to be the secret
of happiness and courage to be the secret of liberty"*
~Louis D. Brandeis

*"Men love their country, not because it is great,
but because it is their own"*
~Seneca

*"Territory is but the body of a nation. The people who inhabit its
hills and valleys are its soul, its spirit, its life"*
~James Garfield

"Ev'ry heart beats true 'neath the Red, White and Blue"
~George M. Cohan

*"We need a type of patriotism that recognizes the virtues of those
who are opposed to us..... The old "manifest destiny" idea ought
to be modified so that each nation has the manifest destiny
to do the best it can - and that without cant, without the
assumption of self-righteousness and with a desire to learn
to the uttermost from other nations"*
~Francis John McConnell

*"I believe in America because we have great dreams - and because
we have the opportunity to make those dreams come true"*
~Wendell L. Wilkie

"To me, being an American means feeling safe"
~Currielene Armstrong

*"We on this continent should never forget that men first crossed
the Atlantic not to find soil for their ploughs but to
secure liberty for their souls"*
~Robert J. McCracken

*"It is sweet to serve one's country by deeds,
and it is not absurd to serve her by words"*
~Sallust

*"We need an America with the wisdom of experience.
But we must not let America grow old in spirit"*
~Hubert H. Humphrey

"May I never wake up from the American dream"
~Carrie Latet

*"A real patriot is the fellow who gets a parking
ticket and rejoices that the system works"*
~Bill Vaughan

*"I think there is one higher office than president and
I would call that patriot"*
~Gary Hart

"My patriotic heart beats red, white, and blue"
~Author Unknown

*"Each man must for himself alone decide what is right and what
is wrong, which course is patriotic and which isn't. You cannot
shirk this and be a man. To decide against your conviction is to be
an unqualified and excusable traitor, both to yourself and to your
country, let men label you as they may"*
~Mark Twain

*"All we have of freedom, all we use or know - This our fathers
bought for us long and long ago"*
~Rudyard Kipling, *The Old Issue*, 1899

*"What we need are critical lovers of America - patriots who express
their faith in their country by working to improve it"*
~Hubert H. Humphrey

*"You cannot spill a drop of American blood without spilling
the blood of the whole world....
We are not a nation, so much as a world"*
~Herman Melville

*"Our hearts where they rocked our cradle, our love where we spent
our toil, and our faith, and our hope, and our honor,
we pledge to our native soil. God gave all men all earth to love,
But since our hearts are small, Ordained for each one spot
should prove Beloved over all"*
~Rudyard Kipling

*"He is a poor patriot whose patriotism does not enable him
to understand how all men everywhere feel about their altars
and their hearthstones, their flag and their fatherland"*
~Harry Emerson Fosdick

*"We have enjoyed so much freedom for so long that we are
perhaps in danger of forgetting how much blood it cost to
establish the Bill of Rights"*
~Felix Frankfurter

*"Patriotism is easy to understand in America -
it means looking out for yourself by looking out for your country"*
~Calvin Coolidge

"We dare not forget that we are the heirs of that first revolution"
~John F. Kennedy

"The American Revolution was a beginning, not a consummation"
~Woodrow Wilson

"Intellectually I know that America is no better than any other country; emotionally I know she is better than every other country"
~Sinclair Lewis

Chapter 14

Discovering Your American Dream it Hasn't Changed, Have You?

"The person who takes no chances generally has to take what is left when others are through choosing."
—Napoleon Hill, Author

"We are told talent creates its own opportunities, but . . . intense desire creates not only its own opportunities, but its own talents"
—Eric Hoffer

As I have mentioned in previous chapters, my beginnings at the game of life and my ability to do well in America was not a pleasant story. I had a $2.00 balance in my check book and I was sleeping in my car in the back of a health club.

I did not have very much, but I had a dream and I knew that there was more around the corner. Looking back, I can see that this experience was a "Rite of passage" for me to lecture and write books to help others see that they too can overcome a less than perfect background.

This chapter is not designed to ignore the tough times, but to encourage you to keep going; all things are possible in America, if you focus and work hard. The best advice I can give you at the start of this chapter is: NEVER divorce your dreams, hang on to them, think about them and plan to do what is takes to put your dreams into motion through pro-active activity that takes you toward the accomplishment of your vision.

In the beginning of this book I quoted *As A Man Thinketh.* Here it is again: "*He who would accomplish little must sacrifice little.* – "*He who would achieve much must sacrifice much.* – *He who would attain highly must sacrifice greatly.*" It is a universal principle to achieving. I have seen so many people in my life that just don't get it when it comes to this process: They want the results without the labor or sacrifice.

As I age, my "American Dream" has been adjusted from time to time. I have adjusted my "Sails" from time to time; what was important ten years ago has moved to another part of my to do list. However, if you got to know me, you would always say "He works hard with passion, conviction and is intensely focused on the goals that he sets." My joy today is the ability to give back and make a difference. I feel that I do that with my books, lectures and educational websites. I will let you in on a little secret; the giving starts the receiving process, unselfishly of course.

As you can tell, I am a big fan of the opportunities we have in America. Let's take a look at this in some detail.

According to the Merriam-Webster Collegiate Dictionary, opportunity is: A chance for advancement or progress.

Another definition is: Favorable time, a break, chance, occasion, opening, and a state of affairs or combination of circumstances favorable to some end.

Opportunity can come in many shapes and sizes: money, promotions, owning your own business, or spending more time with your family. And sometimes, opportunity is right under your feet. Have you ever heard the story of 'Acres and Diamonds?' And this brings my point close to home. There was this farmer in South Africa who sold his farm to travel the world in search of diamonds. Today, that farm that he sold is the site of the largest diamond mine in the world. Sometimes the acres of opportunity are right under your feet.

One of my goals is to help you implement the following four concepts into your life:

1. *Get the most from your current opportunity. That's very important.*
2. *Develop a better game plan and achieve greatness throughout your life.*
3. *Perform to your full potential.*
4. *Go after whatever it is that you want to go after.*

When I was offered a position as manager there was no training, there was also a lot of negative sales talk and a lot of negative feedback, I had no choice at the time, I had $800 in my pocket. I took off in my Grand-Am from North Carolina to drive to Los Angeles for the "Golden opportunity." At that time I didn't know what I couldn't do, I went out and basically had to make things happen, also at the time I knew I had six months to make it or break it. As you can imagine the turnover rate in that managerial position was quite high.

I looked up to the person who had hired me; I took copious notes about what I needed to do to succeed. I put my ego in my back pocket and I knew it was up to me to get the job done.

Basically, they threw me out to the wolves and I didn't walk away. I kept going for several reasons; I wanted to better myself and saw the opportunity to do so, I recognized that if this was the opportunity for me and someone else was doing well why not me? I was not going to lose this great opportunity through lack of hard work. I broke down the opportunity into its components and decided that, "Yes," there was something worth going after and something that I was going to have. I was going to work hard enough to get it and make it happen for me.

As I mentioned earlier, when you're looking to develop yourself for success, you need to first **wake up** and take a personal inventory of who you are. Next, you need to get **motivated**, change your thinking and develop a reason to succeed.

Let's talk about getting motivated. MOTIVATION is something that can be difficult. MOTIVATION is like working out. Everyone wants the perfect body. Everyone wants to be motivated all the time, but how many of us are willing to take the time, the effort and discipline to get up and get the perfect body that we want? MOTIVATION must come from inside you. External MOTIVATION will only work short term. You can get inspiration from external sources, but lasting MOTIVATION is internal. Don't wait for the coach to show up to get motivated, they may never arrive.

To stay motivated takes work and time. Many people claim that they have no extra time, because of the things that they already do. But, how much time do they spend watching television? People in this country, have been fed on TV and fast food. I did not own a TV until five years ago when we built our house.

There was a big blank space on one wall that needed something - what I felt - a nice big screen color television would fit just fine. I only use it to watch DVD's, because commercial television is one of the most negative things out there. I have no disrespect for good educational stations; I'm just not a television fan. I also love DVD's, but TV, is a waste of time, it's negative, because negativity is easier to sell than POSITIVE information.

Rather than spending time watching someone else's negative program, you should be spending time developing your own POSITIVE program. Talking about television, I'm reminded of what Groucho Marx had to say on the subject. He said, "*I must say I find television very educational. The minute someone turns it on, I go to the library and read a great book.*" I love that quote by Groucho; make it a part of your life. Spend more time developing yourself than watching TV.

Many years ago I had an opportunity that I didn't recognize, and at the time I didn't know how to take advantage of it. Would you know an opportunity if it ran across your forehead, or possibly stood right in front of you? That's the first mile to the road to success. The second mile is MOTIVATION. At first I did not succeed because I was unable to get internally motivated. I didn't know what I wanted. I didn't know how to get out of bed and go after those things that I wanted.

I'm going to share with you some thoughts and ideas that will *"Wake you up, get you motivated,"* and get you ***going after*** your dreams day after day, week after week, and year after year. As I mentioned, you have got to get out of bed to get motivated. It seems like I have several sales representatives that have difficulty getting out of bed every single morning. When I talk to them, they're always crying poor mouth. They're broke. They can't pay their bills. They want more out of life, but there are many times that they have called their manager and said, 'Hey, do me a favor, give me a wake up call, would you?'

This is unbelievable! These people are between thirty-five and fifty years of age, and they still need a wake up call. Wake up America! There's something wrong with this picture. If what it takes to get you out of bed is someone holding your hand, you're in trouble. You're in the wrong system. To get out of bed, though, you have got to have a purpose. I talk to a lot of people around the country and it consistently amazes me how so many people lose an opportunity because they have a reluctance to act. I'm here to tell you today that if this is the case, I want you to change. It's a fact that in this world you either deal or get dealt. Don't let fear stop you.

It's that simple.

You must however have a clear picture of your "face" of opportunity, or you will not be able to recognize it even if it is in front of you. Success goes to the marathon runner, not the sprinter!

FIRST: Opportunity should be for the long-term. A good opportunity will advance you in your life; not just for a few months.

SECOND: Check out the "Success credentials" of the person who is offering you that great opportunity. This person should be succeeding at a high level. We become the people with whom we associate most closely. Therefore, associate with successful people to assure your success.

Usually, when you have a high degree of difficulty, you should have a high degree of opportunity. Nothing of true value comes easily.

Determine your own definition of Success.

Know your definition of success. For some people its making a great deal of money; to others it is a company that offers flexible hours; others it is a stress-free environment.

Some studies suggest that people are switching to employment opportunities that offer less income, but offer work that benefits society. Know what you consider important in life, and you will have your own definition of success.

Your definition of success will motivate you.

Know what is important to you in a job opportunity. Maybe money is your main motivation. That's okay. Just make sure you like what you do.

An opportunity is one in which money can be made on a continuing basis; not just for one year. Another important concept defining opportunity is the fulfillment of psychological growth: Will this opportunity offer recognition for your achievements and be interesting to you for many years? Will there be room in the company for your growth and advancement?

Know what the important elements of the job are right for you?

Look at the day-to-day activities of the job. If the minor aspects of a job do not make you happy it will be very hard to stay in the position long-term. For example:

1. An air-conditioned office. Do you prefer working inside or outside? If you feel cooped up in an office then you

should not apply for a position that requires you to stay in the office on a daily basis. If you prefer being outside, then a position which requires you to call on the client, rather than the client coming to you would be better for you.

2. Do you want and need direct supervision, or do you work better unsupervised? Are you self-motivated, or must there be someone watching you before you do your work?

3. Do you want to know what you are going to do every day, or do you prefer variety? Do you like the same routine, or being creative in your work?

4. Do you want to work set hours? Or would you rather work flexible hours, setting your own pace until the work is finished?

The more you know about what's important to you, the easier it becomes to spot Your Opportunity. If you don't know what you want you won't recognize your best choice in a company. Chances are you will make the wrong decision—again!

An article in USA Today reported on what success means to people. Only 25% of adults surveyed said that a lot of money meant success to them. Of the people surveyed, 80% of them said, that control in their life was what mattered the most.

Control in your job can mean controlling your income and how many hours you must put into the job. These are all important factors that must be looked at when looking for a position.

You can see that the right opportunity for one person may not be the right opportunity for another person.

Define what you want in your opportunity.

Many workers seek greater meaning in their work. They want to see that what they do makes a difference in the world; at least in their culture or society; at the very least for an appreciative customer. They would like to go home each day with a sense that they have made some kind of contribution. Management will have to make some changes for this new worker.

The best time to search for your opportunity.

You need the proper techniques for finding your great opportunity, now that you have figured out exactly what you want.

No matter how much you want to change employment, if you are currently employed it can be hard to find time to conduct an extensive job search.

If you are unemployed and worried about paying the bills, it's hard to search for that "opportunity," with financial pressure mounting.

It's easier to find a job when you are employed. Well, maybe this is true, but it's also true that finding the right opportunity is a full-time occupation.

My philosophy is to keep an active income coming in so you don't disturb any investments or financial commitments, and keep your bills paid. It's stressful enough looking for other opportunities.

It amazed me when people who worked for me resigned without having another position. These people had families who relied on them for support: two or three kids. They left their benefits and had nothing whatsoever in the works, but they went ahead and quit.

Your resume represents YOU!

If you have a two-week vacation, take it. Get your resume ready prior to your vacation. Please have it done professionally. I see many unprofessional-looking resumes.

Your resume represents you, it's your introduction to the position you are seeking.

I have received resumes that were handwritten, on lined paper, and/or sloppy. This tells me that the person sending the resume has so little ambition that he or she can't even put together a correct resume. Why would I hire that person?

I have received resumes from people applying for a job in a totally different company or area than was advertised in the ad. Don't waste your time. Those resumes are useless to the recruiter. They are thrown away.

Make sure your telephone number is correct on your resume. Do not forget to include your area code!

Always proofread your resume to make sure the spelling, grammar and punctuation are correct. If spelling and grammar are not your strong points, have it professionally checked. Keep your information current. There are professional resume companies that will compile your resume for you. Use them.

I have seen top decision-makers and top recruiters look at a resume and within two or three seconds throw it into the trash. Spend the money and take the time to get a professional resume put together.

Take your two week vacation to look for a position. If you don't want do to that, then honesty is the best policy: go to your employer and tell the truth, and if you have been a productive employee your boss will understand.

He or she may even ask to part company now and give you a severance package. There may be a placement program within the human resources department.

Caveat! Make sure you know your employer's reactions before you take this path. The risk you take is that your employer will tell you to leave now, without a severance package.

I want you to remain employed. If you decide you can't, then do not leave because you are mad or upset.

Never burn your bridges!

The new company with which you are interviewing will ask you questions to make sure you haven't done anything to any past employers that could affect your future with them.

An acquaintance of mine left a very respectable company without giving them notice. When cutbacks and mergers took place in his current company, they didn't give him notice because they knew of his past behavior. Be careful. Use your head.

Potential employers often ask why you are not employed.

You are on an interview and the employer asks you, "Why aren't you working at present?"

Your answer should be basic:

"When I realized my former employer was not going to take me in the direction I wanted to go, I decided to look elsewhere. I found that I couldn't carry out an effective interview search without neglecting my job. I didn't want to short change my company, so I gave them notice."

This may work or it may not. You owe it to yourself to consider all the risk factors before deciding to resign. Again, let me remind you, you are going to need your former employer to give you a good reference.

Success is the best Kind of revenge!

There is a popular saying, don't get mad; get even. That's a terrible piece of advice! You deserve better counsel!

Get mad (anger can be a powerful motivator, if you keep it under control), but don't get even!

It's okay to get mad if you've lost your job, but don't get even—get ahead!

You have four options when you go into career-decision mode:

1. Work for another company
2. Work for yourself
3. Stay where you are
4. Retire

There are two key factors in a career decision making process:

FIRST: You have to make a decision.

SECOND: You have to make sure the decision you have made is the right decision. To make an effective decision you must do a number of things:

1. Clarify and organize your thinking. Write down your answers to all the questions I've asked in this book.

2. Appraise your strengths and marketability. Know your strengths and how that affects you getting the job you want. If you need more skills in your area, then learn them.

3. Understand your marketplace. Understand your industry and what is going on that is new and forward-thinking. Don't be left behind because you didn't know something you were doing is obsolete.
4. Determine your options. What happens if plan A fails? Have an alternate plan ready.
5. Weigh your alternatives. Is it time to change careers? When the car was invented, many people said it wouldn't last and kept their stock in horses.
6. Develop your action plan and how you will go about implementing it. Give yourself time and date lines.

What is a successful company?

The success of companies depends upon the competence of their people. The 80/20 rule is applicable here (20% of the people do 80% of the work). The most competent people are fewer in number, so when they leave a company a disproportionate amount of corporate strength leaves with them. If too many of the most competent people leave, a company can suffer financially. You can see how valuable you can become to a company.

Sometimes Opportunity Comes as a Kick in the you know what.

Opportunity comes in many guises. It may come as a feeling of discontent with your present job. Your job may vanish. Your company may go under. These circumstances will not necessarily be due to a recession, or anything else that is happening in the economy. No matter where or how you are employed, it may happen in the future that you are going to feel the earth move beneath your feet. The nature of the work you do may be redefined.

If you're in middle management, odds are you are already being shifted into a new kind of leadership role, or have even been thrown out of the system and are looking for a new position.

You've heard terms like re-engineering and reinventing and you've seen all the books and articles about companies downsizing. Unless you've buried yourself in the world of junk television, you've seen symptoms of a great and fundamental change in American corporations: Layoffs, plant closings, cost cutting and benefits slashing. Only 30% of companies offer any kind of pension plan. Many companies are no longer offering medical benefits. It's no accident that one takeover-turnaround CEO (who is admired or reviled, depending on who you talk to), has earned the nickname "Chainsaw" because of his slash-and-burn approach to restoring a failing company to profitability.

These are the reasons why you must develop your skills to the extent that companies will beg you to come work for them— and you will have the delightful option of only working for your choice of the best companies out there, because you have the skills they want.

Whatever changes we go through, modern technology will never replace our most precious asset: the worker.

That's you!

The more valuable you make yourself to a company by learning the necessary skills, the more job protection you have.

If your company should go out of business or your job is eliminated, your skills will be your passport to a better and higher position in another company.

Who is going to help the entrepreneur grow all those small businesses? People. Think before you take the plunge.

A good opportunity is like the stock market: it's meant for the long haul. If you pull your money out too soon you'll lose when the market is down. And if you make a quick decision on a company, you may soon be out looking for a new job again.

"If one person can do something, anyone can." All you need to do is use a successful person as your role model and follow the same steps he or she Used to become successful.

Companies are like relationships— you have to work at them.

If you are in the age bracket between thirty-five and fifty-four, I want you to stay put. I don't want you to jump from job-to-job. This is, of course, after you have found the right opportunity. Try to stay with one thing and make the most of it. Become that competent employee the corporation cannot do without.

What Happens after The great Opportunity?

You are offered a great opportunity. Now what?

Two things have to be set in motion for the opportunity to succeed. I call them labor and discipline. Whatever your opportunity is, you have to labor at it and have the discipline to press on, even when things are not going your way. There is no such thing as easy success.

Discipline and labor combined with the right opportunity equals success.

Discipline is HOW all great accomplishments happen.

Discipline in life is what separates the winners from the losers in any and every area of life. The winners keep going when the losers quit. Anyone who has discipline can achieve success. Discipline is what keeps people going when the inner voice tells them it's too hard. They ignore that inner negative voice and keep going because they see the goal at the end of the hard road. People with discipline do not take the easy way, but keep pressing on when the going gets tough. They make the twenty sales calls till they get a sale; they run the marathon until they finish, no matter how painful the final miles may be. Only you can make the decision.

Are you a winner or a loser? (I get tired of dancing around this question)

People who are not successful usually look at people who have accomplished a lot and put it down to luck. Well my friend, I'm here to tell you that luck has little to do with it. Without discipline nothing in life would be accomplished. Stick with whatever you start and don't stop till you have completed the task. Stay with what you've started even though you experience failure time after time. Eventually, when you stay at something long enough, you will become successful. Most losers in life quit when they experience their first failure. Be a winner. Persevere. Prepared activity will equal results!

Labor goes hand in hand with discipline. You must find out what steps it takes to become successful, and then work at them until you have accomplished your goal, and every day you must do it again and again. Labor never ends. Discipline and labor equal success, combined, of course The Old Axiom: Look for Opportunity in Your Own Backyard.

I know that what we've talked about sounds like a lot of hard work. It is! The key question though.......is it worth it? Will it make a difference? Yes!

Let it be the dream that it used to be. Let's not lose our future through lack of performance, and let's have the courage, optimism, strength and integrity to continue the American LEGACY greatness.

Only you can make that difference; it must start now, and it must start with you, with the right opportunity. We will finish up this chapter with a great quote.

"Press on. Nothing in the world can take the place of perseverance. Talent will not; nothing is more common than unsuccessful men with talent. Genius will not; unrewarded genius is almost a proverb. Education will not; the world is full of educated derelicts.

Persistence and determination alone are omnipotent."

— Calvin Coolidge, thirtieth president of the United States

Chapter 15

The 10 Greatest Entrepreneurs

*"When you reach an obstacle, turn it into an opportunity.
You have the choice. You can overcome and be a winner, or you
can allow it to overcome you and be a loser. The choice is yours and
yours alone. Refuse to throw in the towel. Go that extra mile that
failures refuse to travel. It is far better to be exhausted from
success than to be rested from failure."*
—Mary Kay Ash, founder of Mary Kay Cosmetics

There is a tough truth that any small business owner has to face. Even in the best of times, the vast majority of small businesses fail. We will look at ten entrepreneurs who not only succeeded, but built vast business empires.

John D. Rockefeller

John D. Rockefeller was the richest man in history by most measures. He made his fortune by squeezing out efficiencies through horizontal and vertical integrations that made Standard Oil synonymous with monopoly - but also dropped the price of fuel drastically for the everyday consumer. The government broke up Standard Oil for good in 1911. Rockefeller's hand can still be seen in the companies like Exxon (NYSE:XOM) and Conoco that profited from the R&D and infrastructure they received as their piece of the breakup. Rockefeller retired at the turn of the century and devoted the rest of his life to philanthropy. (More than 70 years after his death, this man remains one of the great figures of Wall Street. Learn more, in J.D. Rockefeller: From Oil Baron To Billionaire.)

Andrew Carnegie

Andrew Carnegie loved efficiency. From his start in Steel, Carnegie's mills were always on the leading edge of technology. Carnegie combined his superior processes with an excellent sense of timing, snapping up steel assets in every market downturn. Like Rockefeller, Carnegie spent his golden years giving away the fortune he spent most of his life building. (Though not as well-remembered as some of his contemporaries, Andrew Carnegie's legacy is strong and moralistic, read The Giants of Finance: Andrew Carnegie.)

Thomas Edison

There is no doubt that Edison was brilliant, but it's his business sense, not his talent as an inventor, that clearly shows his intelligence. Edison took innovation and made it the process now known as research and development. He sold his services to many other companies before striking out on his own to create most of the electrical power infrastructure of the United States. While Edison is a founder of General Electric (NYSE:GE), many companies today owe their existence to him – Edison Electric,

Con Edison and so on. Although Edison had far more patents than he did corporate ties, it is the companies that will carry his legacy into the future.

Henry Ford

Henry Ford did not invent the automobile. He was one of a group working on motorcars and, arguably, not even the best of them. However, these competitors were selling their cars for a price that made the car a luxury of the rich. Ford put America - not just the rich - on wheels, and unleashed the power of mass production in the bargain. His Ford Model T was the first car to cater to most Americans - as long as they liked black. Ford's progressive labor policies and his constant drive to make each car better, faster and cheaper made certain that his workers and everyday Americans would think Ford (NYSE:F) when they shopped for a car.

Charles Merrill

Charles E. Merrill brought high finance to the middle class. After the 1929 crash, the general public had sworn off stocks and anything more financial than a savings account. Merrill changed that by using a supermarket approach - he sacrificed the high commissions to serve more people, making up his money on the larger volume. Merrill worked hard to "bring Wall Street to Main Street," educating his clients through free classes, publishing rules of conduct for his firm and always looking out for the interests of his customers first. (We all know names like Rockefeller, but there are other influential pioneers of finance in America's history, see The Unsung Pioneers of Finance.)

Sam Walton

Sam Walton picked a market no one wanted and then instituted a distribution system no one had tried in retail. By building warehouses between several of his Wal-Mart (NYSE:WMT) stores, Walton was able to save on shipping and deliver goods to busy stores much faster. Add a state-of-the-art inventory control system, and Walton was lowering his cost margins well below his direct competitors. Rather than booking all of the savings as profits, Walton passed them on to the consumer. By offering consistently low prices, Walton attracted more and more business to where he chose to set up shop. Eventually, Walton took Wal-Mart to the big city to match margins with the big boys - and the beast of Bentonville has never looked back.

Charles Schwab

Charles Schwab, usually known as "Chuck," took Merrill's love of the little guy and belief in volume over price into the internet age. When May Day opened the doors for negotiated fees, Schwab was among the first to offer a discount brokerage for the individual investor. To do this, he trimmed the research staff, analysts and advisors, and expected investors to empower themselves when making an order. From a bare-bones base, Schwab then added services that mattered to his customers, like 24-hour service and more branch locations. Merrill brought the individual investor back to the market, but Chuck Schwab made it cheap enough for him to stay. (Learn more in The CEO Dream Team - Walton, Schwab, Marcus and Blank.)

Walt Disney

The 1920s found Walt Disney on the verge of creating a cultural juggernaut. A gifted animator for an advertising company, Disney began creating his own animated shorts in a studio garage. Disney created a character inspired by the mice that roamed his office, Mickey Mouse, and made him the hero of "Steamboat Willie" in 1928. The commercial success of Mickey Mouse allowed Disney to create a cartoon factory with teams of animators, musicians and artists. Disney turned that mouse into several amusement parks, feature-length animations and a merchandising bonanza. After his death, the growth has continued making Disney (NYSE:DIS), and his mouse, the founders of the largest media company on earth.

Bill Gates

When people describe Bill Gates, the usually come up with "rich", "competitive" and "smart." Of the three traits, it's Gates' competitive nature that has carved out his fortune. Not only did he fight and win the OS and browser wars, but Gates stored up the profits that came with the victories – and Microsoft's dominance – to fund future fights and ventures. The Xbox is just one of the many sideline businesses that the massive war chest has funded. The fact is that Microsoft's cash and Gates' reluctance to pay it out is a big part of what saw the company through hard times and funded expansion in good times.

Steve Jobs

Unlike most of the others on this list, it's possible that Steve Jobs' greatest achievements are yet unwritten. Jobs co-founded Apple (NYSE:AAPL), one of the only tech companies to offer a significant challenge to Microsoft's dominance. In contrast to Gates' methodical expansion, Jobs' influence on Apple has been one of creative bursts. Apple was a computer company when Jobs returned to it. Now, the iPod, the iPhone and the iPad are the engines of growth that have pushed Apple past the once unassailable Microsoft. When Apple surpassed Microsoft's market cap in 2010, it became clear to investors that, with Jobs, the best is yet to come.

Conclusion

These 10 succeeded by giving the customer something better, faster and cheaper than their nearest competitors. No doubt, some like Rockefeller will always be on these lists, but there is plenty of room for the right person to find their place among the entrepreneur's pantheon. Source: Andrew Beattie is a managing editor and contributor at Investopedia.com.

Will you be one of the next "Great" Ones?

Everything is Possible in America!

*Shoot for the moon even if you miss
you will be among the stars.*

Chapter 16

Twenty-Steps for Success & Twenty-Six Top Characteristics of Successful People

Success is not easy: Change your Attitude
"All things are difficult before they are easy."
—John Norley

In my years as a business owner, author and speaker, I have witnessed those that have it and those that don't. I am astonished that with all the books and how to programs which are out there that some people still fall short of their personal and professional goals. Included is a list of the twenty-six top characteristics of successful people in America, and twenty steps on how to succeed in any profession. I will also share with you some of my secrets of success.

I started with the U.S. Chamber of Commerce at twenty-five. I stayed with them for fourteen years. I grew each year I was with them.

When I left the Chamber, I was at one of the highest executive levels— and knew there was no longer any more room for my growth.

I knew it was time to start my own consulting company: Winner's Legacy International, Inc. and help other companies achieve their success.

Why did I succeed when so many other sales managers, and other people who were hired by the U.S. Chamber quit or failed.

What were the steps that I took to assure that I held on to my ideal opportunity at that time.

These steps are what I did, and the advice I urge you to take to heart and follow.

ONE: Do not get caught up in the politics of any company you work for. When the company is having a bad time, don't run with the herd and jump ship. I stayed through four restructurings at the Chamber. I had five different bosses. Many of the people I worked with were gone or demoted.

TWO: Don't look back. Get over your "I'll give it a try" attitude; the belief that, "If it doesn't work out, I'll go on to something else, or I'll go back to what I left." What would have happened if Thomas Edison had that attitude? I guess we'd be reading this book by candle light.

My philosophy is, get in or get out.

If what you were doing before was so great, you wouldn't have left. You have obviously taken the steps— interviewed with the present organization two or three times, if not more, and applied my seven step Victory System. You know it's the right move: Stop being flaky. Separate yourself from the masses. If success was easy, everyone would be successful; there would be no first class, and gasoline would be fifty dollars a gallon.

THREE: Commit to what you are doing. Don't keep thinking that success is easy; it is not.

The only place "success" comes before "work" is in the dictionary.

When I started my sales career many years ago I knew it was a great opportunity for me, and I gave it my total commitment. When things got tough, I didn't quit; I worked harder, I stayed focused on what was in front of me.

Moe's story is an example of perseverance and commitment, and living the American Dream. He was a young man from another country. When I hired him, Moe was driving a bus in a small town in Utah. I saw something in Moe. In his first year he became one of the top ten sales representatives—out of 400! Moe earned $70,000 his first year—and he could hardly speak English.

One evening when I was having dinner with him and his wife I asked, "Why have you been so successful?" He said, "I didn't have a choice. Americans have too many choices, Randy. If something becomes too difficult, they just move on to the next thing. I do not have this choice." I'll never forget Moe's answer. And you should not either; I know there's no such thing out there as the perfect opportunity— nothing is perfect. Opportunity does not lie with the position, it lies within you as an individual. Any position you take becomes boring after a few years or even a few months. It's up to you to create the excitement, to keep the position new and interesting by continually learning new skills.

I have a good friend who has been a barber for 20 years. He loves what he does because as he told me he does each haircut as if it were his first.

When I started with the U.S. Chamber, they didn't offer any training. I created training manuals and other tools. I looked to see who was successful. I called them and asked questions. I read books on leadership. I learned what it took to be a successful sales leader. Most important, I persevered. I never gave up. When I hired people, if they wanted to succeed, I never gave up on them. I still follow the same credo: I never give up on myself or on the people I lead. And I am still learning new skills.

FOUR: Study and learn. Whatever it is you're going to do, be the best that you can be. I interview many people who want to change jobs. But before they change jobs I ask them, "Did you get all you can out of your present position?"

You want to be on top in your industry. You can achieve this by studying and learning everything you can about the company, product or service. In this way you will be able to maximize the current opportunity you have. Look at successful people in your industry. Observe what they do to succeed, and do the same. If one person can do it, anyone can. Read the books, listen to motivational tapes, and put in the labor and discipline needed to achieve success.

FIVE: Give 100% of yourself when you are on your job. When I train people or managers I tell them, "There are two things that you must do to succeed. One: you have to work at what you do. Two: you must put in the hours."

- You have to work to succeed. Success doesn't come easy.
- You have to put in the time to become competent and proficient at what you do.
- Discipline weighs ounces, but regret weighs tons.

How many of you have looked back on your life and have said "If only I did this, or maybe if I had done that."

Do not let yourself look back on your life and say you lost an opportunity because you lacked the discipline and didn't work hard enough.

I know that if you work hard and give it all you have, then we will be able to count you among the top one or two percent of people within your company. People in my company think I'm talented, that I have some kind of special gift.

I have discipline and I work hard.

SIX: Number six has paid me the highest dividends throughout my career. Stay positive through thick and thin. I know this is hard, but believe me, it works.

You may not feel positive inside, but never show negativity to your boss or to your fellow workers.

I worked with Harry, a sales manager who was doing a fairly good job. The company let him go because of his negative attitude. Harry would put a damper on any new idea that was proposed, and people had a hard time being around him.

When the company restructured, Harry was let go. They told him, it was because of his poor attitude and not being a team player.

It's not going to be a bed of roses, day in and day out. You are going to have rough times as well as good times, but through it all, stay positive. All the tough times I've had in my career, when I look back, were not as bad as they seemed at the time. I look back today and laugh.

SEVEN: Don't gossip. When I would go to the Chamber's regional office, 80 to 120 people were working there. It's easy to start gossiping; what's this, what's that, who's here, who's there. I find that when I get caught up in this idle gossip I feel negative. I am more productive not getting caught up in the negativity of office gossip.

EIGHT: Add value to your employer. Become an asset and not a liability. In Japan, people practice Kaizen. Kaizen is the philosophy that every employee is expected to improve their job performance, find a way to cut costs in a company, and to improve on the product the company sells. This is job security—you become so valuable to your company, because of what you add, that they would never think of downsizing you. It feels good to become a valuable person where your ideas are wanted and respected.

Throughout this book I mention two very important factors: Good people are hard to find, and good companies are hard to find. When you find that great company, become an asset. When times get tough and the company has to look where to cut, they will cut only their liabilities. You, as an asset, have job security.

NINE: If you work hard at your job, you will make a living. What I really want you to do is to work harder on yourself—and you will make a fortune. The job you are looking for, or are in right now, will take you only so far intellectually and financially. You must put in the time to study and educate yourself apart from your job. Learn another language, another culture. Intel encourages its people to travel and study other cultures. As I mentioned earlier in the book, Intel gives their people two months off to travel and learn after seven years with the company. You have to look at the big picture of who you are. This way you won't stagnate as a person or in your job. You'll become energized and fired up. That equals an improved life all around. Work harder on yourself than you do on the job.

TEN: Don't ask what you are getting from this opportunity; ask what are you going to become. What are you becoming? Many people make big money, but they may not be good people. All they can do is make money. So what?

There are other people who don't make much money, but they contribute to society. They have become great people through what they do.

ELEVEN: Never quit. Stay with it. Many times we think, "I'm going to quit. I'll go on to something bigger and better."

But, chances are, something bigger (or merely different) is not better. Most successful people, including me, stayed at something. Stay till you succeed. It's no fun being unemployed.

TWELVE: Show up early and stay late. Try to be the first in the office and the last to leave. Make your boss look good. Many times, the boss doesn't have the answers. A good boss will surround himself or herself with competent, quality people who do. When the boss is promoted, you go with him or her; or the boss recommends you. I don't have all the answers, but my management team is not afraid to make me look good. They know that they benefit.

A good boss will make sure that you are taken care of. I sometimes hear people say that they could do things better than their boss, or they always make their boss look good and he doesn't give them any recognition. I would suggest to these people they look for a new boss.

THIRTEEN: Dress professionally. I don't care what the dress code is—business is business. People gravitate toward winners. You look like a winner when you are dressed professionally. If you are not sure how to dress professionally, imitate the successful people in your company. Go to the bookstore and read a book on how to dress. Find out where the sharp professional people buy their clothes, and shop there. Get the best haircut you can afford. Don't forget to shine your shoes.

FOURTEEN: Act as if you owned the company you work for. Pick up trash you didn't create. Handle things that come up that are not in your department. Take pride in your company. Make their problems your problems. Don't let your company fold because nobody was taking care of the clients.

Take leadership.

FIFTEEN: Give more than you get. If you help enough people get what they want, you will have all that you want. Start giving more than you receive. It will come back to you many times over.

SIXTEEN: Have fun. I'm on the road 180 nights a year, on airplanes, in airports, away from my wife. I have to have fun at what I do. No matter what happens, no matter what takes place, I have fun. Money cannot be your prime motivation. You may make $300,000 a year, be miserable, and end up losing your family. You would take out your misery on your family when you got home and they would throw you out.

Please have fun!

When you're having fun, little things won't get you down. Remember, this is not a life or death situation; this is a career. Many people live for weekends. I love my weekends, but I can't wait for Monday. I look forward to going to work. Whatever you do in your career, make it fun.

SEVENTEEN: Go for it. Whatever it is you're getting ready to do, or are doing currently; go after it with all your energy, commitment, and desire. Don't lose the promotion or position because you didn't go after it. You will get 90% of what you want from your employer just by asking.

EIGHTEEN: Dream big.

Dream bigger than you think possible. Without a dream you will not get there. But you must have a flight plan. Use my Victory System as your flight plan. Remember shoot for the moon even if you miss you will still be among the stars.

NINETEEN: Keep growing. You must grow spiritually, emotionally, psychologically, and health wise. Devise goals for all areas of your life. Don't neglect your health while trying to get ahead in your career. Otherwise you won't be around to enjoy it. Put time aside for your spiritual side. Thank whatever higher power you worship for your life. Don't forget to be grateful for what you have now—while your eye is on the future.

Enjoy the process. It's getting to your goal that's fun. I guarantee that once you get there, you will say,

"Okay, now what?" And look again for new challenges and rewards. That's okay. It's called growth.

Grow emotionally. Be able to admit your mistakes. Listen

when others say things you don't like, without reacting. Be kind to others, and especially to yourself. Forgive other people for their wrongs against you. It will free your mind. Above all, forgive yourself.

TWENTY: Take leadership.

I cannot repeat or emphasize this enough.

Take the lead on things. Don't wait for someone else to do it. Become the point person. Any time the boss looks around for a leader, let it be you. When you show that you have the ability to lead people and to take on projects in the company, you will advance in the organization.

Everything is possible in America!

26 point Check list

1. Passion	2. Purpose
3. Creative	4. Integrity
5. Initiative	6. Character
7. Dream Big	8. Hard Work
9. Innovative	10. Persistence
11. Clear Vision	12. Independent
13. Self-Confident	14. Have a Mentor
15. Inquisitiveness	16. Expert in a Field

17. Strong Leadership and Organizational Skills

18. High Energy Level	19. Tolerance for Failure
20. Calculated Risk Taker	21. Problem Solving Skills
22. Goal Oriented Behavior	23. Positive Mental Attitude
24. Effective Communication	25. Commitment to Excellence

26. Dream the Impossible

How many of the top 26 do you Possess?

Take a quick test to see which group you fall under.

0 to 10: _____ -you need serious help

11 to 18: _____ -you are on your way

19 to 26: _____ -you are in the top 2%

Seek out the first group and show them the way

Chapter 17

Young Americans and Politics: They are the Future

"The future promise of any nation can be directly measured by the present prospects of its youth."
—President John F. Kennedy, February 14, 1963

While writing and doing research for my book, I looked at many documents that had some amazing statistics about the knowledge of young voters and other interesting findings. I do not want to slant the readers view on what is best for America, I want all who read my book to make up their own minds, or at least continue their own search for what is best. Too many media outlets want you to see things their way. Presenting the facts is hard for most. This is why I have included a chapter such as this one. There are many sources here and as you read you can go and do your own research and come up with you own conclusions as to "What is Best for America?"

Young Voters: An Emerging Political Force

Conventional wisdom in the political community is that young people don't vote, so why target them?

Conventional wisdom, however, is outdated. Consider the facts:

Young adults are huge in number and growing. There are 42 million 18~29 year olds eligible to vote in the U.S., one~quarter of the entire electorate. By 2015, "Millennial Generation" voters between 18~38 years of age will make up one~third of the electorate and be the biggest, most diverse generation in American history.

Today's young adults are paying attention to politics and increasingly likely to vote. In 2004, turnout among 18~29 year olds jumped by nine percentage points, more than twice the turnout increase of the overall electorate. **Over 4.3 million more 18–29 year olds cast ballots in 2004 than in 2000, for a total of 20.1 million voters.**

Young voters will turn out to vote IF you ask them. We know that youth~targeted mobilization campaigns work, particularly with this new generation of more engaged young adults. Further, polling shows that both parties have a stake in turning out different groups of young voters. With their huge numbers, young adults can make the difference in close elections. In the long run, studies show that voting and partisanship are habits that, if developed early, tend to last throughout life.

Given that the Millennial Generation will be one~third of the electorate in less than a decade, today's young voters are essential to building your party for the future. The question then becomes – how do we mobilize young voters?

Demystifying the Youth Vote

The term "youth vote" can conjure a number of (mis)impressions, from the infamous "boxers or briefs" interview to a vague notion of a kid who cares more about the drinking age than about health care, schools or jobs.

This analysis of young voters' political attitudes helps correct these misimpressions. The fact is that young adults are quite similar to the overall electorate in many ways. **Voters 30 and under consistently rank jobs and the economy, education, energy and health care as the most important issues for our elected officials to address, and also show a strong interest in issues of national security and the war in Iraq. They want candidates to reach out to them, to talk about these issues in ways relevant to their lives, and to ask for their votes.**

Of course, today's 18~30 year olds are also a new and different generation in many ways. This generation is more technological-ly~savvy, more diverse, more mobile, and more global than any in U.S. history. This analysis also includes a briefing on the news and communications habits of the Millennial Generation and a summary of the group's demographics, both important factors to consider when targeting and mobilizing today's youth vote.

Youth Politics History

With roots in the early youth activism of the Newsboys and Mother Jones' child labor protests at the turn of the 20th century, youth politics were first identified in American politics with the formation of the American Youth Congress in the 1930s. In the 1950s and 60s organizations such as the Student Nonviolent Coordinating Committee and Students for a Democratic Society were closely associated with youth politics, despite the broad social statements of documents including the liberal Port Huron Statement and the conservative Sharon Statement and leaders such as Dr. Martin Luther King, Jr. Other late-period figures associated with youth politics include Tom Hayden, Marian Wright Edelman and Bill Clinton.

"Our answer is the world's hope; it is to rely on youth. The cruelties and obstacles of this swiftly changing planet will not yield to obsolete dogmas and outworn slogans. It cannot be moved by those who cling to a present which is already dying, who prefer the illusion of security to the excitement of danger. It demands the qualities of youth: not a time of life but a state of mind, a temper of the will, a quality of the imagination, a predominance of courage over timidity, of the appetite for adventure over the love of ease."
- Robert F. Kennedy, South Africa, 6-6-1966

In the 2008 presidential election, 52 percent of registered voters between ages 18 and 29 voted, according to the Center for Information & Research on Civic Learning and Engagement, breaking a history of low turnout.

YDA (Young Democrats of America) provides research and statistics to our chapters to help make the case for investing in youth voting programs. Below are some highlights of the best research on youth voting currently available.

<u>Young Voters they Are a Large, Growing, and Diverse Voting segment.</u>

Commonly called the Millennial Generation or Generation Y, young voters rival the Baby Boomers in size and are the most diverse generation in history.

- Millennials will be nearly 45 million strong in 2008.
- By 2015, this generation will make up one-third of the electorate.

- Voters ages 18-29 were 21% of the electorate (41.9 million) in 2006.
- 39% of Millennials identify as non-white, making them the most diverse generation in American history. Young Latinos account for the largest percentage of the population boom.
- The vast majority of young people are not in college; in fact, only an estimated 25% of 18-24 year-olds attend a four-year college full time.

Between 22 and 24 million young Americans ages 18–29 voted, resulting in an estimated youth voter turnout (the percentage of eligible voters who actually cast a vote) of between 49.3 and 54.5 percent, according to an exit poll analysis released Nov. 4 by CIRCLE, a nonpartisan research center at Tufts University. This is an increase of 1 to 6 percentage points over the estimated youth turnout in 2004, and an increase of between 8 and 13 percentage points over the turnout in the 2000 election. The all-time highest youth turnout was 55.4 percent in 1972, the first year that 18-year-olds could vote in a presidential election.

According to Declare Yourself's survey, 37 percent of voters said that they primarily look for a presidential candidate who agrees with them on the issues. This is also different from surveys in years past, in which respondents have traditionally cited character as a more important attribute of a presidential candidate than agreement on political issues, according to a Nov. 6 Declare Yourself press release. The national issue cited as most important to the largest group of voters was prices/cost of living (33 percent), followed by jobs (13 percent), education (11 percent), and health care (9 percent). Those issues cited by the least number of voters were terrorism (2 percent) and racism (1 percent).

Will young people continue their allegiance toward the election process?

Of the respondents in the Declare Yourself survey, 61 percent said they will be more active in politics in the future, while only 2 percent said they would be less active; 37 percent said they will participate the same amount.

The Freechild Project has found that around the world there is a growing interest in young people participating in politics. Some political groups are changing to respond to the growing number of young people who want to affect the political system. Political ideologies that were once considered "fringe" beliefs are becoming mainstreamed, and more young people are associating themselves with non-popular political parties. Finally, more young people than ever before are actually becoming engaged in local community campaigns and other political activities.

Point to Ponder

"Nobody will ever deprive the American people of the right to vote except the American people themselves-and the only way they could do this is by not voting."
-Franklin D. Roosevelt

Resources

The following categories have been identified by Freechild to help young people and their adult allies learn more about young people & politics. There are several categories with headings.

Organizations Promoting Youth Voting[11]

- **League of Pissed Off Voters** - Create social support to strengthen families. Foster a spirit of shared responsibility and community. Bring all voices into the public dialogue. Protect our right to privacy and our freedom of choice. Make real opportunities available to all. Use government to invest in the public good. Be a respected and respectful citizen of the world. The most important youth engagement program of 2004.

- **Mobilizing America's Youth** - An all-partisan network dedicated to educating, empowering, and energizing young people to increase our civic engagement and political participation.

- **Canadian Youth Politics** - A discussion board for young people in Canada.

- **Millennial Politics.com** - Dedicated to educating and motivating people about youth activism. Hosts active discussions about youth activism and politics, publish a weekly newsletter to over 650 people about youth activism and are writing a book about the activism of our generation.

- **Teen Power Politics** - "Silence is the door of consent." Information, resources and inspiration to do something.

- **Youth Lobbying Organization** - Provides the structure through which high school students will have their opinions heard on issues concerning themselves and their peers.

- **Vote Smart** - A nonpartisan record of which candidates voted for what.

- **Kids Voting USA** - Kids Voting USA is a nonprofit, non-partisan, grassroots organization dedicated to securing democracy for the future by involving youth in the election process today.

- **Youth Vote** - Youth Vote is the nation's largest non-partisan coalition working to increase the political involvement of 50 million Americans, 18-30 years old. The Youth Vote coalition consists of over ninety diverse national organizations representing hundreds of organizations and millions of young people.

- **Rock The Vote** - Organization begun by members of the recording industry dedicated to promoting freedom of expression and the empowerment of young people. Engages youth in political advocacy and encourages voter registration.

- **Young Citizens Survey** - A survey of 1,500 Americans between the ages of 15 and 25. Young adults are more positive today about government, their communities, and their own civic and political involvement -- but those attitudes have yet to translate into action. Young adults are an "unclaimed constituency," looking for candidates for public office to come to their turf, take them seriously, and ask for their votes. These are some of the key findings of the most comprehensive survey of young people today, containing a wealth of new information about their attitudes toward, and participation in, politics and civic life.

- **Youth Vote Coalition** - The nation's largest non-partisan coalition working to increase the political involvement of

50 million Americans, 18-30 years old. The Youth Vote coalition consists of over one hundred diverse national organizations representing hundreds of organizations and millions of young people.

- **Youth in Action** - Provides support and recognition for the voices, ideas and positive solutions of youth. As partner in the Global Youth Action Network, a growing collaboration among organizations worldwide, the youthlink.org web site is being expanded as an international clearinghouse for youth voices, resources and action.

- **Third Millennium** - Advocates for the Future - Third Millennium is a national, non-partisan, non-profit organization focusing on long-term problems facing the United States, such as the national debt. The organization conducts research, publishes opinion articles, and testifies before Congress. Its stated goal is to "inspire young adults to action."

- **Young Politicians of America** - The Young Politicians of America was founded to expand the democratic experience to the youth of our society. The problems community service aims to answer are the same problems government seeks to solve. Our goal is to further citizenship among young people by catalyzing their zeal for community service into a zest for civic participation. Through YPA chapters, young people volunteer, discuss, and encourage each other to understand government's role as a crucial instrument for impact.

- **Lowering the Voting Age** - Resources and information about lowering the voting age and promoting youth suffrage across the United States.

- **Green Party Youth Caucus** - The Greens give official recognition, including a direct voice in county, state, and national committees, to organized caucuses of Greens who are members of oppressed groups. Includes the following for youth: proportional representation; guaranteed parity; affirmative action; right to caucus; recognition of Youth caucus.

- **Libertarian Party Campus (Youth) Information** - Libertarians believe the answer to America's political problems is the same commitment to freedom that earned America its greatness: a free-market economy and the abundance and prosperity it brings; a dedication to civil liberties and personal freedom that marks this country above all others; and a foreign policy of non-intervention, peace, and free trade as prescribed by America's founders.

- **Student Natural Law Party Club** - The Natural Law Party was founded in April 1992 to "bring the light of science into politics." Its founders, a group of a dozen educators, businessmen, and lawyers, knew that field-tested solutions to America's problems already existed but were being ignored by government, due primarily to the pervasive influence of special interests.

- **Young Democrats** - The Young Democrats of America (YDA) has been the official youth arm of the Democratic Party since 1932. Open to anyone under the age of 36 who affiliates with the Democratic Party, YDA is a nation-wide grassroots organization with 42 chartered states and 780 local chapters. Our 43,000 plus membership reflects the broad diversity of our nation and the Democratic Party. This includes high school students, college students, young workers, young professionals and young families. All of the members have the interest of their community at heart and work hard to affect the democratic process.

- **YROCK** - The Young Republicans Online Community network - Today's Young Republicans are young professionals between the ages of 18 and 40, who belong to a nationwide network of like-minded individuals. The Young Republican National Federation, Inc. is the governing body that oversees the State organizations across the country and facilitates opportunities for Young Republicans to have an active role in politics today. Members of Young Republican clubs not only benefit from the social aspects, but the chance for future political development. As America's farm team of Republican politics, the YRNF has spent the last 70 years creating the leaders of today, as well as training the next generation for tomorrow.

- **Political Parties for Youth**

- **Party Y** - Party Y is a coalition of young American leaders (all in their 20s) who joined together in 2002 to launch a new independent political youth party dedicated to meeting the needs of America's under-30 population. Not a traditional "third party", we are instead a web/media-based "virtual party" designed to link up young voters with equally young political candidates (all under-30) around the country.

- **The Future Voters of America Party, Inc. (FVAP)** - A New York City based program founded in 1995 as a not-for-profit political party for youth and now in its fourth year with youth involvement. The FVAP will provide an American political home that unites young people on youth-centered issues, promotes active citizenry, and fosters life-long patriotism and national spirit.

"We will not deny, we will not ignore, we will not pass along our problems to other Congresses, to other Presidents, and other generations."
—President George W. Bush, January 28, 2003

Chapter 18

Great Achievements by Teenagers

"You can do whatever you dream of and become inspired
if you stay focused, work hard and don't give up.
You will raise above 95% of your classmates"
—Randy E. King

Teenagers throughout history have had many great achievements in the fields of art, culture, science and technology. This may be because they are able to think in new and innovative ways, or their thinking is not hidebound by discredited nostrums; it may be attributable to great teachers and great schooling - including homeschooling. It may simply be the emergence of God-given talent at an early age. Biologically the rate of brain development and according to some studies IQ, reportedly peak in smart individuals just prior to their teenage years.

Achievements, listed by age at which they were made

- Age 7 - Yehudi Menuhin gives his first solo violin performance with the San Francisco Symphony in 1923.

- Age 8 - Frederic Chopin plays his first public piano performance, having already authored two polonaises (G minor and B flat major) at age 7.
- Age 10 - Mark, author of the Gospel of Mark, witnesses the arrest of Jesus and develops the first Gospel.
- Age 10 - Michael Kearney, homeschooled, becomes the world's youngest university graduate. At age 17, began a teaching career at college.
- Age 12 - Blasé Pascal had secretly worked out the first twenty-three propositions of Euclid by himself.
- Age 12 - Jesus presents His wisdom in the temple in Jerusalem.
- Age 12 - William "Willie" Johnson earned the Medal of Honor for his actions during the Seven Days Battle and on the Peninsula Campaign during the American Civil War.
- Age 13 - Jonathan Krohn homeschooled, actor, internet radio host, guest speaker at CPAC, author of Defining Conservatism.
- Age 13 - John wrote the first draft of the Gospel of John, the greatest written work of all time.
- Age 13 - Joan of Arc was inspired and led France five years later to victory over the English in the Hundred Years War; was martyred at age 19.
- Age 13 - Anne Frank began writing her diary, later published as "Anne Frank: The Diary of a Young Girl."
- Age 14 - Ismail founded the Safavid dynasty and became its "shah" (military and spiritual ruler).

- Age 14 - Bobby Fischer became an International Chess Grandmaster.
- Age 14 - Mozart wrote the opera, "Mitridate Rè di Ponto."
- Age 14 - Nadia Comaneci "achieved in her sport what no Olympian, male or female, ever had before: perfection."
- Age 14 - St. Theresa of Lisieux rejected by Bishop Hugonin, pleads with Pope Leo XIII so she may enter the Carmelites. Became Carmelite nun at age 15.
- Age 14 - Bernadette Soubirous (St Bernadette of Lourdes) has a vision of the Virgin Mary.
- Age 15 - Louis Braille invented the Braille system.
- Age 15 - Christopher Paolini writes the first draft of his Eragon trilogy which is published when he is 19.
- Age 16 - Jean-François Champollion, can speak a dozen languages and delivers a paper on the Coptic language to the Grenoble Academy. By 20, he can speak another 13 languages and at 32 he deciphers the Rosetta Stone.
- Age 16 - Boy sailor Jack Cornwall, of HMS Chester, is awarded a posthumous VC for gallantry at the Battle of Jutland.
- Age 16 - Roger Mason discovered the first fossil believed by paleontologists to come from the Ediacaran period (630-542 million years ago). He found the fossil in Charnwood Forest, Leics, UK. The fossil species is named Charnia masoni, in recognition of his contribution to geology and evolutionary biology.

- Age 16 - the average age of 58 homeschooled teenagers who founded Conservapedia, so that the light of truth would continue to shine and darkness would not overcome it.
- Age 17 - Cassie Bernall defended her faith in front of an atheistic gunman at the Columbine massacre, and was martyred for it.
- Age 17 - Mary accepts God's will to conceive Jesus by the Holy Spirit, and gives birth nine months later.
- Age 17 - Shawn Fanning develops the first large-scale peer-to-peer file sharing program, Napster.
- Age 17 - Private 1st Class Jacklyn H. Lucas, United States Marine Corps, earned the Medal of Honor five days after his 17th birthday during the Iwo Jima battle in World War II; he was a Marine for three years.
- Age 18 - Shawn Goldsmith from Long Island has earned all 121 merit badges offered by the Boy Scouts.
- Age 18 - Mary Shelley writes Frankenstein (The Modern Prometheus), later published when she was 21.
- Age 18 - Gary Kasparov, considered the greatest chess player ever, won the U.S.S.R. championship.
- Age 19 - Captain Albert Ball, VC, MC, DSO & 2 bars, commences his career as a fighter pilot. By the time he is killed, aged 20, in 1917, he has become one of the First World War's greatest air aces, accounting for at least 44 German aircraft.
- Age 19 - was the average age of front-line US service personnel fighting to defend democracy in Indochina during the Vietnam War.

GREAT ACHIEVEMENTS BY TEENAGERS   305

- Age 19 - Evariste Galois develops group theory, and wrote it out completely on the eve of his death at age 20; it took old mathematicians a century to comprehend it.
- Age 19 - John D. Rockefeller starts a new company, turning an enormous profit in its first year, and became the most influential businessman in history.
- Age 19 - Steve Jobs begins collaborating in electronics with Steve Wozniak in electronics, and developed the personal computer within two years.
- Age 19 - Mark Zuckerberg develops Facebook, the leading social networking system for young people on the internet.
- Age 19 - Jim Ryun broke the world record for running the mile.
- Age 20 - Carl Friedrich Gauss makes his first mathematical discoveries, which will lead to the completion of "Disquisitiones Arithmeticae," his magnum opus, at the age of 21.
- Age 20 - Willis Carrier invents air conditioning.

What are you going to do and when?

Go to www.storiesofusa.com and tell us your story and your dreams or accomplishments. You could be in our 2nd edition of this book.[12]

Chapter 19

Realizing What You Have

"It is one of the most beautiful compensations of this life that no man can sincerely try to help another without helping himself."
—Ralph Waldo Emerson

I am going to tell you about capitalizing on the American opportunity and jump starting your own success process. The three key areas in developing your success process are: ***Waking up***; ***Getting motivated***; and ***Going after it***.

Waking up is: Developing an awareness process, so that you can take a viable, personal inventory of your abilities and evaluate your current opportunity.

KEY POINTS

- If you want to develop to your full potential, put your ego in your back pocket. You must take a fearless inventory of your strengths and your weakness.
- Put opportunity first, dollars second.
- Opportunity is not on the outside, it is within the individual.

- Positive affirmation without discipline without action leads to disillusion.
- Recognize and evaluate what's in front of you. Determine if your current situation will allow you to meet your current goals.
- Never fall short due to lack of hard work.
- If you want more out of life, you must be willing to do whatever it takes to succeed.
- Don't take advice from someone who is more messed up than you are.
- Learn more to become more.
- Ask yourself, "Am I an asset or a liability to society?"
- Is what you are currently doing moving you toward or away from your goal?
- Evaluate your foundation in all areas of your life.
- Are you maximizing what you can do every day?

Now getting motivated means: Instituting a self-improvement program and developing a sense of MISSION about your life's activities.

KEY POINTS

- Motivation is internal and it takes work and time.
- Deal, or get dealt. Activity plus effort equals results.
- You must decide to be POSITIVE about life.
- Develop pride of ownership.
- Discipline weighs ounces, regret weighs tons.
- Develop passion and purpose for your work.
- Adopt your company's MISSION statement.

- Adopt no excuse living.
- Don't look for shortcuts for success.
- Ask for help; find a mentor.
- Hone your skills and improve your self-esteem.
- Make productive things your priority.
- Make a difference "Now."
- Develop a personal game plan to stop bad habits.

Going after it is what I consider the final step in maximizing opportunity. Here you elevate yourself by helping others and implementing Legacy Leadership.

KEY POINTS

- Start thinking like a leader.
- Develop a personal legacy and "pass on" your gifts.
- Develop a personal mission statement.
- Develop a personal betterment program.
- Balance - find yourself a positive escape.
- As a leader, serve people.
- Become a living success example for others to follow.
- Help your community and children grow.
- Share overcoming your own failures to lead other people.
- Successful leadership involves solving problems.
- Be thankful for the difficulty levels in life.
- Change yourself, and not the world.

I know that what we've talked about sounds like a lot of hard work. It is! The key question though, is it worth it? Will it make a difference? Yes!

It's like the old story about the man who came upon a second man at the sea shore. Littering the beaches were countless starfish. The second man was busy throwing the starfish back into the sea, and upon reaching the second man the first man asked him, "Why are you bothering to throw the starfish back into the sea? There are so many that you possibly can't make a difference." To which the second man replied as he tossed another starfish back into the sea, "It made a *difference* to that one."

Now, I have one final thought before I leave you, because if we don't pay attention, our greatness our freedom and our American way of life will be in trouble. As Langston Hughes said, **"*We must let America be America again.*"**

Let it be the dream that it used to be. Let's not lose our future through lack of performance, and let's have the courage, optimism, strength and integrity to continue the American LEGACY of greatness.

Only you can make that difference; it *must* start now, and it must start with *you*!

God bless this great country - Go out and grab what life and America has to offer.

Chapter 20

What Is Next for America?
It all depends on you-

"He who knows much about others may be learned, but he who understands himself is more intelligent. He who controls others may be powerful, but he who has mastered himself is mightier still."
—Lao Tzu

During my research and writing of my book, I found a lot of statistics, facts and figures in which I found myself many times shaking my head in disbelief. So what I ended up doing was using only what I considered relevant data: some points, facts and articles that I thought would fit and add value to the reader. I want this book to have time tested relevancy which can be re-read over time. But, I could not resist putting in the following information because it applies very much now and in the future.

Five Myths about Those Civic-Minded, Deeply Informed Voters

1. You hear this one from politicians all the time, even John McCain, who promises

Straight talk, and Barack Obama, who claims that he's not a

312   LEFT – CENTER – RIGHT, WHAT IS BEST FOR AMERICA?

politician (by which he means that he'll tell people what they need to hear, not what they want to hear). But by every measure social scientists have devised, voters are spectacularly uninformed. They don't follow politics, and they don't know how their government works. According to an August 2006 Zogby poll, only two in five Americans know that we have three branches of government and can name them. A 2006 National Geographic poll showed that six in ten young people (aged 18 to 24) could not find Iraq on the map. The political scientists Michael Delli Carpini and Scott Keeter, surveying a wide variety of polls measuring knowledge of history, report that fewer than half of all Americans know who Karl Marx was or which war the Battle of Bunker Hill was fought in. Worse, they found that just 49 percent of Americans know that the only country ever to use a nuclear weapon in a war is their own.

True, many voters can tell you who's ahead and who's behind in the horse race. But most of what they know about the candidates' positions on the issues and remember, our candidates are running to make policy, not talk about their biographies derives from what voters learn from stupid and often misleading 30-second commercials, according to Kathleen Hall Jamieson, director of the Annenberg Public Policy Center.

2. Bill O'Reilly's viewers are dumber than Jon Stewart's.

Liberals wish. Democrats like to think that voters who sympathize with their views are smarter than those who vote Republican. But a 2007 Pew survey found that the knowledge level of viewers of the right-wing, blustery "The O'Reilly Factor" and the left-wing, snarky "The Daily Show" is comparable, with

WHAT IS NEXT FOR AMERICA? IT ALL DEPENDS ON YOU- 313

about 54 percent of the shows' politicized viewers scoring in the "high knowledge" category.

So what about conservative talk-radio titan Rush Limbaugh's audience? Surely the ditto-heads are dumb, right? Actually, according to a survey by the Annenberg Public Policy Center, Rush's listeners are better educated and "more knowledgeable about politics and social issues" than the average voter.

3. If you just give Americans the facts, they'll be able to draw the right conclusions.

Unfortunately no! Many social scientists have long tried to downplay the ignorance of voters, arguing that the mental "short cuts" voters use to make up for their lack of information work pretty well. But the evidence from the past few years proves that a majority can easily be bamboozled.

Just before the 2003 invasion of Iraq, after months of unsubtle hinting from Bush administration officials, some 60 percent of Americans had come to believe that Iraq was behind the Sept. 11, 2001, terrorist attacks, despite the absence of evidence for the claim, according to a series of surveys taken by the PIPA/Knowledge Networks poll. A year later, after the bipartisan, independent 9/11 Commission reported that Saddam Hussein had nothing to do with al-Qaeda's assaults on the World Trade Center and the Pentagon, 50 percent of Americans still insisted that he did. In other words, the public was bluntly given the data by a group of officials generally believed to be credible and it still didn't absorb the most basic facts about the most important event of their time.

4. Voters today are smarter than they used to be.

Actually, by most measures, voters today possess the same level of political knowledge as their parents and grandparents, and in some categories, they score lower. In the 1950s, only 10 percent of voters were incapable of citing any ways in which the two major parties differed, according to Thomas E. Patterson of Harvard's Kennedy School of Government, who leads the Pew-backed Vanishing Voter Project. By the 1970s, that number had jumped to nearly 30 percent.

Here's what makes these numbers deplorable and in fact, almost incomprehensible: Education levels are far higher today than they were half a century ago, when social scientists first began surveying voter knowledge about politics. (In 1940, six in ten Americans hadn't made it past the eighth grade). The moral of this story: schooling alone doesn't translate into better educated voters.

5. Young voters are paying a lot of attention to the news.

Again, no. Despite all the hoopla about young voters -- the great hope of the future! -- Only one news story in 2001 drew the attention of a majority of them: 9/11. Some 60 percent of young voters told Pew researchers that they were following news about the attack closely. (Er -- 40 percent weren't?) But none of the other stories that year seemed particularly interesting to them. Only 32 percent said that they followed the news about the anthrax attacks or the economy, then in recession. The capture of Kabul from the Taliban? Just 20 percent.

Six years later, Pew again measured public knowledge of current events and found that the young (aged 18 to 29) "know

WHAT IS NEXT FOR AMERICA? IT ALL DEPENDS ON YOU- 315

the least." A majority of young respondents scored in the "low knowledge" category the only demographic group to do so.

And some other statistics are even more alarming. How many young people read newspapers? Just 20 percent. (Worse, studies consistently show that people who do not pick up the newspaper-reading habit in their 20s rarely do so later). But surely today's youth are getting their news from the Internet? Sorry. Only 11 percent of the young report that they regularly surf the Internet for news. Maybe Obama shouldn't be relying on savvy young voters after all.

Rick Shenkman is an associate professor of history at George Mason University and the author of "Just How Stupid Are We? Facing the Truth about the American Voter."

Hopefully by this point your mind is racing ninety miles per hour! I hope that is the case. Getting you to think for yourself and to become aware as to what the facts are and what sensationalism media hype is! The information is out there for you to learn and educate yourself on the real facts. As Ronald Regan stated "Informed patriotism is what we want." America is worth the effort. Staying positive and focused on what is truly best for you will most likely be what is best for America. It truly is about "Winning Strategies, Thoughts & Inspirations." I love the " If it's to be its up to me," that says to me that I can make a difference, not only for myself, but also my family and those around me who I come in contact with every day.

America will stay the great nation that is today. It is all our choice and I get fired up about that option. The ability to come and go, pick and choose, and to create our own America is essential to longevity of our freedoms, prosperity and democracy. And most importantly the ability to "pass it on" to our young Americans.

Being an informed citizen, aware of issues that affect you and having knowledge of your personal and political philosophy is essential for the education process and democracy to work. We all agree that not getting caught up in the media hype, and taking personal leadership within the election process with the understanding of who and what is right for you will certainly ensure America's greatness! So, with all that said, it truly is our Country and it still continues to be your Choice.

Now, to answer the sub-title of this book's question: **"What is Best for America?"**

YOU ARE!

"For tomorrow belongs to the people who prepare for it today."
-African Proverb

About the Author

Randy King for over twenty-five years has been active with America's small business community. He was a senior leader with the world's largest business association for fourteen years.

After leaving the association Randy founded his own software and consulting companies. Randy's consultation with a seventeen Billion dollar energy company resulted in a 600% gain in sales within sixteen months.

Randy has also consulted with the National Federation of Independent Business (NFIB) the nation's most influential small business advocacy group.

Throughout Randy's career, he has been the keynote speaker and advisor to many fortune 500 companies on performance and development of their staff. He has been interviewed on hundreds of talk radio shows nationwide and internationally. Randy has shared the speaking platform with congress and various elected officials. Randy frequently is asked to speak before business groups throughout the nation. He also is a faculty member at one of the top university based leadership academies.

He is an international author with seven business/leadership books. He produced and authored a children's eBook on what America means to our youth. He has four audio education programs and several "White Papers" on personal performance. He is the co-author of the world renowned, www.storiesofusa.com an interactive multi-language site for young Americans to understand the history of our American Heritage.

His lectures, books and educational site and overall message has been received and viewed by over 90% of countries throughout the world.

He lives in Arizona with his wife Linda, and their famous Doberman, Miso (He is the one on the back cover with me; I had to bribe him with lots of cookies to do the shoot!)

Quick Order Form & Contact Information

Thoughts – Comments – Questions

Contact Road Scholar Publishing Group:

     Email: Reboh@cox.net or call: 602-549-9833

     Email orders: reboh@cox.net

     Telephone orders: CALL 800-913-1359

     Fax orders: 480-515-0489. Send this form

Please send more FREE information on:

    ☐ Other books

    ☐ Speaking/Seminars

    ☐ Consulting

Name:_____

Address:_____

City:_____State:_____Zip:_____

Telephone:_____

Email address:_____

The Author is available for

interviews – lectures and book signings

Also, charity events for your school/Non-Profit

Organization or Civic/Business group

Email the author @ rking23@cox.net

he enjoys hearing from his readers!

Resources

1. Wikipedia.org
2. U.S. Dept. of Labor, Bureau of Labor Statistics, Business Employment Dynamics; Advocacy-funded research by Zoltan Acs, William Parsons and Spencer Tracy, 2008 (www.sba.gov/advo/research/rs328tot.pdf).
3. U.S. Dept. of Commerce, Census Bureau and Intl. Trade Admin.; Advocacy-funded research by Kathryn Kobe, 2007 (www.sba.gov/advo/research/rs299tot.pdf) and CHI Research, 2003 (www.sba.gov/advo/research/rs225tot.pdf); U.S. Dept. of Labor, Bureau of Labor Statistics.
4. The Impact of Regulatory Costs on Small Firms, an Advocacy-funded study by Nicole Crain and Mark Crain, 2010
5. U.S. Dept. of Commerce, Census Bureau, Survey of Business Owners; Advocacy-funded research by Open Blue Solutions, 2007 (www.sba.gov/advo/research/rs291tot. pdf), and Office of Advocacy: The Small Business Economy (www.sba.gov/advo/research/sbe.html).
6. www.school-teacher-student-motivation-resources-courses.com

322   LEFT – CENTER – RIGHT, WHAT IS BEST FOR AMERICA?

7. http://www.acce.org/index_ektid1128.aspx
8. Information Please® Database, © 2007 Pearson Education, Inc.
9. Sources:
    World English Dictionary
    Dictionary.com
    Merriam-Webster's Dictionary of Law
10. All quotes sourced from www.quotegarden.com
11. WinningCampaign.org
    Polling Young Voters was compiled by Young Voter Strategies, a project of the Graduate School of Political Management at The George Washington University with support from The Pew Charitable Trusts.
12. Conservapedia.com

References for speeches

- Give Me Liberty or Give Me Death by Patrick Henry – March 23, 1775
  Source: http://libertyonline.hypermall.com/henry-liberty.html
- The Decision to Go to the Moon by John F. Kennedy – May 25, 1961
  Source: http://www.jfklibrary.org/Historical+Resources/Archives/Reference+Desk/Speeches/JFK/003POF03Spac
- Pearl Harbor Address to the Nation by Franklin D. Roosevelt – December 8, 1941
  Source: http://www.americanrhetoric.com/speeches/fdrpearlharbor.htm

- I Have a Dream by Dr. Martin Luther King – August 23, 1968

  Source: http://www.usconstitution.net/dream.html
- Blood, Toil, Sweat and Tears by Winston Churchill – May 13, 1940

  Source: http://www.historyplace.com/speeches/churchill.htm
- The Right of the People to Rule by Theodore Roosevelt – March 20, 1912

  Source: http://teachingamericanhistory.org/library/index.asp?document=1125
- Inaugural Address of John F. Kennedy – January 20, 1961

  Source: http://www.americanrhetoric.com/speeches/jfkinaugural.htm
- Duty, Honor, Country by General Douglas MacArthur – May 12, 1962

  Source: http://www.americanrhetoric.com/speeches/douglasmacarthurthayeraward.html
- First Inaugural Address of Franklin D. Roosevelt – March 4, 1933

  Source: http://www.americanrhetoric.com/speeches/fdrfirstinaugural.html
- Farewell Address to the Nation by Ronald Reagan – January 11, 1989

  Sources: http://www.americanrhetoric.com/speeches/ronaldreaganfarewelladdress.html

- Farewell Address – George Washington – December 23, 1783
  Source: http://www.earlyamerica.com/earlyamerica/milestones/farewell/text.html
- Remarks at the Brandenburg Gate by Ronald Regan – June 12, 1987
  Source: http://www.americanrhetoric.com/speeches/ronaldreaganbrandenburggate.htm
- Abraham Lincoln's Gettysburg Address – 1863
  Source: http://americancivilwar.com/north/lincoln